Simple Faith?

*Cycle B Sermons
for Lent/Easter
Based on the Gospel Texts*

John B. Jamison

CSS Publishing Company, Inc.
Lima, Ohio

SIMPLE FAITH?

FIRST EDITION
Copyright © 2014
by CSS Publishing Co., Inc.

Published by CSS Publishing Company, Inc., Lima, Ohio 45807. All rights re-
served. No part of this publication may be reproduced in any manner whatsoever
without the prior permission of the publisher, except in the case of brief quota-
tions embodied in critical articles and reviews. Inquiries should be addressed
to: CSS Publishing Company, Inc., Permissions Department, 5450 N. Dixie
Highway, Lima, Ohio 45807.

Library of Congress Cataloging-in-Publication Data
Jamison, John B., 1952-
    Simple faith? : cycle B sermons for Lent-Easter based on the gospel texts /
John B. Jamison. -- FIRST EDITION.
        pages cm
    ISBN 0-7880-2799-9 (alk. paper)
    1. Bible. Gospels--Sermons. 2. Lenten sermons. 3. Easter--Sermons. 4. Common
lectionary (1992). Year B. I. Title.
    BS2555.54.J36 2014
    252'.62--dc23

                                                                2014014832

For more information about CSS Publishing Company resources, visit our web-
site at www.csspub.com, email us at csr@csspub.com, or call (800) 241-4056.

e-book:
ISBN-13: 978-0-7880-2800-7
ISBN-10: 0-7880-2800-6

ISBN-13: 978-0-7880-2799-4
ISBN-10: 0-7880-2799-9   PRINTED IN USA

*This book is for Pat, Tricia, Michael, Ben, and Emily,
with a heartfelt thanks to all of the storytellers
who have guided me in the journey.*

Table of Contents

Introduction

The lesson that took me the longest to learn was to just get out of the way. Once I realized that my preaching was not about me, or about my needing to explain what was meant in the various chapters and verses, my preaching began to change. I began to view myself as just another storyteller, with the privilege of being able to retell some of the most powerful stories in the world. If there is to be any impact of my preaching, it is from the stories themselves, rather than from me. So what follows are my attempts to offer approaches to retelling some of those stories. If you want to add more to them to fit your situation, please feel free, but I encourage you to keep the focus on the stories themselves.

If you find anything that you believe is improper or offensive in my retelling of any story, please understand that it was not intentional. I have the greatest respect for these stories but I also feel it is important to try and tell them in ways that might have more meaning today. As I prepare, I see my listeners as intelligent people, having intelligent worries, and asking intelligent questions. I've found that the old stories can stand up to any questions or challenges, if we just let them do so. But, if any of my language makes you uncomfortable, just rewrite those pieces to create your own version of the story for your listeners.

In a few instances, I have suggested some possibilities for how the message might be presented a bit differently. Whether you use those suggestions or not, the stories will still speak for themselves.

Finally, I hope you enjoy re-hearing this little collection of stories as much as I have enjoyed hearing them again myself.

Ash Wednesday
Matthew 6:1-6, 16-21

Beware of practicing your piety before others in order to be seen by them; for then you have no reward from your Father in heaven. So whenever you give alms, do not sound a trumpet before you, as the hypocrites do in the synagogues and in the streets, so that they may be praised by others. Truly I tell you, they have received their reward. But when you give alms, do not let your left hand know what your right hand is doing, so that your alms may be done in secret; and your Father who sees in secret will reward you. And whenever you pray, do not be like the hypocrites; for they love to stand and pray in the synagogues and at the street corners, so that they may be seen by others. Truly I tell you, they have received their reward. But whenever you pray, go into your room and shut the door and pray to your Father who is in secret; and your Father who sees in secret will reward you. And whenever you fast, do not look dismal, like the hypocrites, for they disfigure their faces so as to show others that they are fasting. Truly I tell you, they have received their reward. But when you fast, put oil on your head and wash your face, so that your fasting may be seen not by others but by your Father who is in secret; and your Father who sees in secret will reward you. Do not store up for yourselves treasures on earth, where moth and rust consume and where thieves break in and steal; but store up for yourselves treasures in heaven, where neither moth nor rust consumes and where thieves do not break in and steal. For where your treasure is, there your heart will be also.

Actors

Whenever you give alms, do not sound a trumpet be-fore you as the hypocrites do in the synagogues and the streets....

We can almost see the people in the crowd leaning for-ward as they try to hear these things Jesus was saying that afternoon on the hillside. He had been talking for a while now, and although he started out talking about things that were theological, he was now getting to things that actually made sense to everyone. It was nice to hear him say how the poor are actually blessed, and the weak will one day inherit the earth, but while those ideas are comforting, they are re-ally kind of hard to make any real sense of in the day-to-day things that go on.

He was talking about things that were real, like praying, giving, and fasting. These are things that everyone deals with and often struggles with, so they all leaned in a bit more to see if he had anything to say that might really mean something.

Many of us are familiar with these words and the after-noon that Jesus spoke to the crowd on that hillside by the Sea of Galilee. We've talked a lot about it and have even given it a name: *The Sermon on the Mount*. We know some parts better than others, like that list of things that are blessed that we call the Beatitudes. Since we've been here before, let's take a step back from what is being said here and take a little different look at things to see if we can hear anything new in this story.

In your imagination, picture that crowd of people sitting on the grassy hillside next to the lake; you can close your eyes if it will help. We see Jesus standing down by the shore in that cove where his voice would carry up the hillside so everyone could hear him. It's actually a very pretty place: the water from the lake calmly lapping against the shore, a nice breeze blowing in from across the lake carrying the smells and sounds of a peaceful day. Every once in a while there is the sound of a wooden oar hitting the side of a boat as the fishermen go about their day on the lake, oblivious to what was going on there on the side of the hill.

Like in the movies, begin to pull the camera back from that hillside, slowly zooming back to take in more and more of the scene. We can now almost see the entire crowd, spread across the hillside, much larger than we might have actually expected. It is a colorful crowd and near the back edge of the group you can see children running around and playing games after becoming bored with all the talking that was going on. There are animals, some carts, all of the things you would expect with a large group of people traveling to a big event.

As the camera pulls back, we see that the little hillside is on the north side of the Sea of Galilee, and we can see the western and eastern shores beginning to curve to the south. Most of us expect the Sea of Galilee to be much larger than it actually is, with all of the things that happened around it, but actually it is not large at all. You can easily see across it from east to west. The hillside with the crowd is just a short walk from Capernaum, where Jesus and the disciples have been staying for a while. Another short walk to the east is Bethsaida, the home of the brothers and a busy fishing village. There are several small villages on the western side too, and the city of Tiberias is just out of sight further south. It was only a couple hours' walk, but the odds are that no one here had ever been there before; it was a city built by Rome and not a place most folks from around here cared to visit.

Before we go any further, on the top of the hill just north of where the crowd is listening to Jesus, we can clearly make out the highway. This is one of the busiest roads in the country, stretching from Egypt all the way to Damascus and beyond. People traveling this road come from every country imaginable, and it's likely that some of those travelers would stop for a while to listen to the conversation on the hillside today too.

As our camera continues to move back, at the south end of the lake we can see the Jordan River stretching to the south. This is the bottom edge of Galilee and marks the northern boundary of the land known as Samaria. As we know, Samaria is also not a place where a good Jew wants to spend time. Since coming back from that exile years ago, the Jews and Samaritans have not been good neighbors. In fact, the quickest route from Galilee to Jerusalem in the south is to go through Samaria. But instead, the Galileans would travel east, across the Jordan into what is some really nasty and dangerous roads, just to avoid bumping into a Samaritan. If a Galilean did make the journey through Samaria and happened to walk across a Samaritan's yard, the Samaritan would run outside with a handful of straw, throw it on the spot the Galilean touched, and set it afire to burn away any trace of that Galilean. No, they weren't good neighbors. This is the reason people laughed so hard when they heard Jesus tell that tale about the "good Samaritan." Everyone knew there was no such thing. Surely he was not serious.

Finally, as our camera moves further back, we see the southern edge of Samaria, which is the northern border of the place known as Judea, with its main city of Jerusalem. It might help to picture this whole region of Palestine as having two lands that are Jewish, Galilee in the north and Judea in the south, with the district of Samaria dropped right in between them. But be careful with any assumptions you might make from there. Although we think of Galilee and Judea being parts of the same land that Jesus was to travel, they were actually very different places at that time. If we understand more about that, we'll begin to understand more about Jesus and what was about to happen after that little hillside speech.

People in the land of Judea saw themselves as the only "true" people of the faith. Jerusalem was the center of the world, and the temple was the center of the city. We know they didn't like Samaritans but it's also important to know that they did not care much for Galileans either! To Judeans, Galilee was filled with religious lunatics, political rebels, and people who did not follow the temple traditions. The idea that a messiah might come from Galilee was as foolish as finding that good Samaritan. "Can anything good come out of Galilee?"

And, to be honest, Galilee did deserve a bit of that reputation, though not to the extent the Judeans nurtured it. While Judea was being governed by Rome, Galilee had avoided that direct control and as a result enjoyed a much more independent atmosphere. Many of the people who had strong anti-Roman feelings had fled to Galilee, and many made it their base for planning occasional attacks against Romans, many times in Judea. The Galileans also had a less strict view of the religious rules from the temple in Jerusalem. After all, it was difficult to follow rules that required you to visit the temple every week, when you had to travel all the way across Samaria to get there, so the religious rules were a bit less strict in Galilee.

As a result, Galilee also had a fair share of religious leaders who openly opposed the temple and its rules, and who called for the overthrow of the temple and Rome. There is a list of these acclaimed messiahs coming from Galilee in the years before Jesus, each of whom were eventually arrested and killed.

As we begin to zoom our camera back up north to that spot on lakeshore where Jesus was speaking to a crowd on the hillside, we have to understand that this event was not a new thing. This was Galilee. The only real question most people had in their minds as they listened today was whether or not this guy was any different than the last ones. They all started out strong, promising to get rid of Rome and to get rid of the temple, recruiting men and swords to do the work that God wanted them all to do. None had been successful so far, but maybe this time?

And that's why the Judeans had made the trip up to hear Jesus as well. You can see them standing up near the front of the crowd, where they are easily seen by those attending. Those were the religious leaders and the keepers of the faith. The Sadducees came to listen for any harsh words about the temple and its rituals. The Pharisees came to listen for anything that might violate the laws from the sacred Jewish writings. They stood in the crowd with the Zealots who were hoping for another call to arms for battle against Rome, with the foreign travelers who were just curious, and with the poor, common people who were just living in hope.

This is where it gets interesting. Let's zoom in really close on the Judeans.

Watch them squirm as Jesus says that part about "… whenever you give alms, do not sound a trumpet before you, as the hypocrites do" (v. 2). The Judeans actually did that. When the important people went to the temple to give their offerings, they paid someone to stand and blow a trumpet so everyone knew they were giving it. The more you paid, the better trumpeter you got, and the better it made you look. Keep in mind, if one good trumpeter was an indication of your level of importance, several trumpets playing together just had to be even better. Yes, it was noisy at times.

"And whenever you pray, do not be like the hypocrites who stand in the synagogues and street corners" (v. 5). The temple laws said that when you prayed you needed to stand and face Jerusalem. If you lived in Jerusalem, you stood and faced the temple. These folks were the ones who actually went outside and stood in the street when they prayed, so everyone knew they were good temple rule-followers. Standing proudly on the street corner, colorful robes blowing in the breeze, they'd be surrounded by a seven-piece brass section. And keep in mind, according to some historical documents there may have been as many as 10,000 of these religious leader types living in Jerusalem at this time, each with their favorite street corner.

"And when you fast, do not look dismal like the hypocrites do" (v. 16). The temple rules said that fasting was done as a sign of suffering, to show how sorrowful you were for your sins. The more sorrowful you look, the more miserable the fasting looks. These guys hired make-up artists to make them look really, really dismal when they were fasting, just like an actor would do. Fasting was a common ritual at the time, so there were plenty of opportunities to spruce yourself up in your best "I'm miserable" outfit and enter the competition.

In fact, to help make his point sink in, we're told that Jesus called these people "hypocrites," but the word he used actually meant actor. What he actually said was, "Don't be like those actors who are pretending to be something they're not!" You can be sure that everyone turned to stare at the Judeans as he said it. This was not the type of visibility they had come here seeking.

People had come to hear Jesus, expecting to hear another rebel attempting to overthrow the world. Instead, they heard someone say that the things of the world just don't really matter all that much and really aren't worth worrying about. He said they should not count on how faithful you *look* to have any lasting value, but count on how faithful you *are* in your heart.

This was new. It was very clear to that little group from Judea that this teacher was also far more dangerous than any of the others who had come before, even if it *was* happening in Galilee. So, as Jesus continued talking, while most of the people in the crowd listened closely, those guys from Judea, the Sadducees and the priests, had slowly moved to the back of the crowd where they were huddled together, talking about just what they were going to do about this preacher.

Before we end our story, let's switch our view one last time. This time, pan your camera very quickly across the country and around the globe, until it focuses right here, right on this church, in this place, on this crowd of listening people. The camera is now on us.

We have also come for a variety of reasons. Some have come because this is where you are supposed to come on Ash Wednesday. Some have come to see if there is anything interesting going on. Some have come praying to find hope: some word or some act that will help you find an answer, or help your faith feel more real. Regardless of why you are here, keep the following words in your mind as you leave.

Ash Wednesday is fifty days before Easter, created to mark the beginning of a period of time for us to reflect as well as to look at our faith and the role it plays in our day-to-day lives. Sure we talk about the more "theological" things like salvation and resurrection, but it's also a time for us to remember the more routine things Jesus talked about and did; like those things he talked about on that hillside by the lake.

We're challenged to look at how we use our faith in our daily lives. Is our faith fueling our roles as "actors," helping us say and do the things a pretender would say and do? Or is our faith a part of our life that actually influences how we treat other people, and what we personally believe are the most important parts of our lives? As we go through this season of Lent together, we're going to look more closely at the stories of our faith. Be brave enough to ask questions that come up as we hear those stories and look underneath the complicated doctrines on which we sometimes spend our time focusing. Our challenge is to see if we can hear what Jesus was really saying and doing and what was really going on during those three years of his ministry. It was very real; and it is still very real.

Our Lenten journey is a challenge to us, just as Jesus' ministry was a challenge to those in his day.

Do not be like the actors, who stand up and dress up, pretending to be something they are not. The "oohs" and "ahs" they hear during their performance are the only rewards they will ever get. Instead, be real. Give and pray without making a show. No one but God needs to know you have done it. Instead, remember that over time we usually do end up finding the treasure we seek in our lives; just make sure it is the treasure that your heart truly needs.

Lent 1
Mark 1:9-15

In those days Jesus came from Nazareth of Galilee and was baptized by John in the Jordan. And just as he was coming up out of the water, he saw the heavens torn apart and the Spirit descending like a dove on him. And a voice came from heaven, "You are my Son, the Beloved; with you I am well pleased." And the Spirit immediately drove him out into the wilderness. He was in the wilderness forty days, tempted by Satan; and he was with the wild beasts; and the angels waited on him. Now after John was arrested, Jesus came to Galilee, proclaiming the good news of God, and saying, "The time is fulfilled, and the kingdom of God has come near; repent, and believe in the good news."

Simple Faith?

It all sounds so simple. It's just so nice, so easy, and so straightforward; almost comfortable. And we've heard the story told so many times that many of us know it by heart.

"This John the Baptist guy was standing in the middle of the Jordan River, yelling at people and baptizing them. He was yelling at some of the priests who didn't like him, when suddenly Jesus stepped out of the crowd, walked into the water, and stood next to John. At first, John wanted Jesus to baptize him, but finally, he went ahead and baptized Jesus. There was a dove, and a voice saying that Jesus was God's Son, then Jesus left to go into the desert for forty days and didn't do much more until he heard that John had died."

It actually does sound fairly straightforward, doesn't it? But the problem with stopping here is that it really makes the entire story look "simple," and "easy," and almost "comfortable." And that ends up creating the image many people have that being a person of faith is also going to be "simple," and "easy," and almost "comfortable." Or it seems to say that people of faith are some special kind of people who never have problems and never have doubts or struggles when times get rough. Then, when things are not simple, easy, or comfortable and peaceful in our lives, we immediately begin to question our faith: "What am I doing wrong? Where has God gone? Why is God doing this to me?"

Let's see what we find if we take a fresh look at this comfortable little story. We'll not try and harm it or pull the rug out from under anything but simply try and understand more of what was really happening on that day in the Jordan River valley.

Jesus woke up that morning and rolled up his sleeping mat just as he had done for as long as he could remember in that same place. Nazareth was a fairly peaceful little town, in a fairly peaceful part of the country, known for not a lot more than just being a fairly peaceful kind of place. The area around Nazareth had more than 100 little towns and cities that had been around for a very long time. None of them were even mentioned in passing in any of the religious writings, history books, or stories. It was a place where people lived out their days, doing the things they did. It's where Jesus grew up and lived most of his life.

We don't know much of anything about what Jesus did during that time. Some say he was a carpenter, while others argue he was a stone mason. We actually don't have any clear evidence for either of those possibilities, so either career might have been right. We also don't know much of anything about his family living in Nazareth. Some say there is evidence that he had brothers and sisters, and some suggest he may even have been married. Again, we have no clear evidence for any of this, but if we think about those possibilities in his life, whether or not he did have that larger family connection in Nazareth really doesn't change anything in what happens later.

Overall, we just don't know what Jesus had been doing for all those years in Nazareth, and what it might have been that led him to make the decision he made on that morning. Had he been following John's actions for a long time? The gospel story suggests they were cousins, so it is fully possible that they had kept in touch, or that Jesus had at least been watching John's activities closely. How long had Jesus been thinking about making this step in his life? Had he gotten up on other mornings thinking about going or was this just a sudden step he decided to take on this day? Did he lie awake all night thinking about what might happen, about what it would really be like to leave his life in Nazareth and never be able to come back to it? Or was this something he had planned and he had just been waiting for the right moment to take the step to begin his ministry? We simply don't know.

What we *do* know is that Jesus left his home that morning and walked several hours from the green hills of Nazareth to the southern end of the Sea of Galilee, where John had been drawing a crowd as he preached his message against the temple and the Romans, telling everyone that "the time has come!" I wonder how long Jesus stood in the back of the crowd listening and watching before he stepped forward. What he was about to do was neither "simple," nor "easy," and not in the least bit "comfortable."

Did he spend some time just looking at the priests John was yelling at and the others who had come from Jerusalem? I wonder if he "sized-them-up," thinking about the arguments that were to come. I wonder if he hesitated for a moment as he thought about the power that those people actually held and the role they would play if he kept going forward. I wonder if he was like me and had images of a simpler life flash through his mind, with the thought that it still wasn't too late to just step back away from the crowd and just go home.

If I had been Jesus, I would probably have been arguing with myself during the entire walk from Nazareth. Am I sure this is what I want to do? Why me? I know exactly what has happened to the other people who stepped forward and began preaching in Galilee; they were hung on trees... every one of them. Every time the path came to a crossroad I know I would have hesitated for a moment to consider what life might be like if I took that path instead of this one. Or what if I just went back home?

We know that Jesus had thoughts like these later, when he was praying in the Garden of Gethsemane. He said: "My

Father, if it is possible, let this cup pass from me" (26:39). Was that really the first time he had the thought? Or, as he stood there by the river, knowing that once he stepped forward there would be no way to ever go back, did he quietly pray: "My Father, if it is possible, couldn't I just go back home now?"

Have you ever been in that kind of situation? It might not have been quite this dramatic, with the stakes so high, but can you recall a time when you were faced with one of those decisions that was sure to change things in your life? Maybe it was a career change or a relationship change. Maybe it was the struggle to take a visible stand for or against something you felt strongly about. Perhaps it was a decision to change a behavior or to change an attitude. Perhaps it was a decision to have that medical test or to reach out for help for something. Whatever it was, can you recall the mix of feelings you experienced as you faced that decision? There is a feeling of excitement about the fact that you could take the step and do something that might actually change things that would lead to something new and joyful. That is matched by the good feeling that comes from knowing that you actually *did* something, and didn't just sit back and stew about it any longer. But there is also the realization that taking the step is most likely going to bring about a lot of other changes, some of which could be unpleasant and even quite painful. You realize that once you make the decision, you can't unmake it, and you can never go back to the way things were. While things may not be the way you want them now, you may have the ability to make the choice to change the way things are. You may also say to yourself that sometimes a known situation is better than an unknown one, even if the known situation isn't all that great.

Can you see Jesus standing there in the crowd by the Jordan River with all of these same thoughts running through his head? We have to keep in mind that with everything else we remember and say about Jesus of Nazareth, he was fully human. It should not surprise us that he could have stood there thinking as much about going back home as going into the water, and it should not appear to be discrediting who he was to suggest that he might have had questions, fears, and doubts. Throughout the rest of his ministry, Jesus continually reminded people of just how difficult it actually was to have real faith. It was like passing a camel through the eye of a needle.

All of this is just to say that when Jesus took that first step into the muddy bank of the River Jordan and was seen as a "person" and not just a part of the "crowd," that was a difficult step. It was a step that meant his future was redefined on the spot. He would never go back to Nazareth to be what he had been thus far in his life.

As the water from the Jordan soaked into his robes and John made his proclamation about who Jesus actually was, changes were put into motion that we are still feeling the impact of here today. We're told Jesus heard a voice to affirm the decision he had made. The priests and others from Jerusalem added Jesus' name to their list of possible threats and hurried home to hatch their plans concerning how they would "contain" him. The common people in the crowd became excited because they now had a new religious leader, and someone they could go to with their questions and problems. The radical Zealots in the crowd became excited that they now had someone who would pull them together, pick up the sword, and lead the revolution against Jerusalem and the Romans.

Let's not forget about the many in the crowd who were there because they were followers of John, and who believed that *he* was the one God had chosen to lead the people to freedom. Who was this Jesus who seemed to be taking over and replacing John? We have to remember that, regardless of anything else, these were people who had built their faith around John, and it would be quite some time before they would look at Jesus as anything other than a usurper, someone trying to steal John's role and authority.

Let's pause again briefly at another point in the story, one that rarely gets talked about. It's that moment after the baptism, after the strange sound from heaven, and after they all stepped out of the water and were back on shore. Can you imagine that scene for a minute?

John's disciples were yelling and complaining. The common folk were pressing in close to ask Jesus questions and to see what he was going to do for them now that he was clearly the key religious leader in Galilee. The Zealots were gathered in a group, looking at Jesus and nodding and smiling with grins on their faces. And the gang from Jerusalem was gathered in the background, asking everyone just who this Jesus from Nazareth really was, trying to determine their plan for putting an end to the obvious threat he was creating, by whatever means necessary.

Is it any wonder that the next line in the story says that Jesus "immediately" went out into the wilderness and stayed for forty days? It might have been as much of an escape as anything else; a brief escape from the reality of the new world that had been created simply by his having made the decision to step forward.

The story picks up again when John is killed, and we're told that Jesus then came back and began his active preaching ministry. But before we go on with that part of the story, we really ought to take a few minutes and look more closely at that visit to the wilderness. It is actually more than an escape. The gospel writers refer to it as a time of "tempting," and make it sound like some kind of initiation rite, or a test Jesus had to pass before he could begin his ministry. But we might begin to think differently about it as we recall the many times, later in his ministry, that we're going to find Jesus taking off to spend time in the wilderness, sometimes alone and sometimes with his disciples. Are all of these "tests," or is there something else going on with Jesus and the wilderness? And, if so, is there something here that might have meaning for us as well?

First, let's make sure we understand what we mean when we talk about that wilderness. There was actually a part of the land on the eastern side of the Jordan River that was known as "the Wilderness." It was an extremely harsh land with little water and that meant there was very little of anything else there other than sand, rocks, barren hills, and all of the things that came with those. Wild animals roamed, usually very hungry and looking for something to eat. People did not live in the wilderness, simply because people *could not* live in the wilderness. If anyone was able to survive for any length of time in the wilderness, over two or three days for example, it was only because God helped them survive. The wilderness was not a place where people relied upon themselves or upon anyone else to help them survive. Life in the wilderness was a life of faith alone.

From the earliest chapters of the Old Testament, there is a constant conflict between the stories of the wilderness and the stories of the city. In these stories, the city represents the places where people began to believe they could take care of themselves and did not need to fully rely upon others, or upon God to survive. It was in the cities where people lost their faith and began to believe in themselves or in other powers to live. They believed in things like money, armies, kings, and temples: things that were created by people and which promised life at its fullest.

If you browse through the Old Testament stories, you'll find that the stories about the wilderness are about people struggling and suffering, until God finally appears and renews their faith and their lives. Stories taking place in the city are stories about corruption, murder, evil leaders, and corrupt priests. Finally, the city-people flee to the wilderness where they eventually find God once again, and life is restored. The prophets almost always came from the wilderness and looked and acted like "wild" men. God is in the wilderness, not in the city. If you want to find God, you have to spend time in the wilderness.

Jesus heading to the wilderness was not just an escape, or some kind of a test or time of temptation. The city was the place that tested and tempted faith, not the wilderness. God speaks in the wilderness, reminding us that God does not use our human achievements for any form of salvation, and our real "new beginnings" happen when we are away from those city influences.

Jesus made the decision to accept the call to his ministry. He was heading off to seminary to spend time coming face-to-face with the faith that was going to have to carry him through some unimaginable challenges in his new life. He was not being tested, but was being prepared. It was in this time away from every possible help from anything man-made that he developed the faith that would lead him forward.

It's unfortunate that we've pretty much forgotten what the wilderness is all about. We've seen it as something to stay away from at all costs. Anytime we see someone going through a time of wilderness experience, or anytime we go through the wilderness ourselves, we see it as a terrible thing, and something we need to try to fix as quickly as possible. We send cards, we offer prayers, hoping to somehow pull them back out of their wilderness into a more comfortable place.

We do all spend time in the wilderness at times; there is no way around it. We all have those periods in life when we feel as if we are far away from the comfortable life, experiencing pain and discomfort, alone, with no one to help us and nothing around us to help us feel better or more secure. We're not sure that we can get through another day. We begin to wonder what we have done to deserve this suffering in the wilderness. We ask, "Why is God punishing me, or why is God testing me again?" And we begin to wonder what kind of a loving God would put his children through this kind of testing anyway. Does God really love us? Does God really love *me*? Is there actually a loving God out there somewhere? Once we start down that path of questions about the wilderness experience, there's no stopping it. If God is... then why?

But throughout history, as in today's story, we're reminded that God is in the wilderness, not in the city.

Jesus chose to go to the wilderness, just as he chose to step into the river. He could have stepped out of the water, started preaching, and begun arguing with those priests. But he knew he wasn't ready. He had faith, at least enough faith to make the decision to move forward. He also knew that he was not ready for what was really going to happen. He understood the power of the wilderness and the strength he would find by taking some time to trust only in his faith and confront what it meant to be totally on his own with that faith, so he went to "wilderness school."

Something quite amazing happens when we begin to look at our own wilderness times as something other than punishments, or tests, or empty suffering. No, they still never become fun or easy, or even something that we would ever actually choose to experience, as Jesus did. But when we realize that even in those darkest, most desolate times, we are never actually alone, and we have not been "sent" there by some god who has left us to suffer and fend for ourselves. We realize that it is in those wilderness times that we have the best opportunity to hear God's voice, above the din and hustle of the routine of life in the comfortable city. We realize that the wilderness is a temporary time, a time that can actually deepen our faith and our love for life, rather than destroy them. Then, perhaps, can we survive the wilderness experience and come back to the city ready to live life to the fullest.

As the story continued, John was arrested and killed, and Jesus understood this as the signal that the time had arrived for him to step up once again. "School" was over. He walked from the wilderness, facing a long list of choices yet to be made, but with the understanding that no matter what those choices might bring, his faith would survive. That is a life of faith.

The Lenten journey is a time to reflect. Suppose we reflect a few moments on the wildernesses in our lives; those times that just barge in and interrupt our lives, scare us, make us feel alone, make us feel angry, make us feel helpless, make us feel… hopeless? What if? Just what if those are the times that God is standing the closest to us, speaking in a very calm and quiet voice? It is a voice that we just don't hear when everything is going the way we think it should go and we're just sailing through life focusing on all of those important things! What if those horrible, painful, miserable times of our lives are not some form of punishment, or failure, or proof that there is no God, and that life is generally rotten.

But what if these times are just a normal part of life and a part of the cost of being human? And what if these wilderness times are the times that truly prepare us to live life to the fullest, to learn how to make the choices that need to be made, and to do the things that need to be done in order to live a life of faith?

Lent 2
Mark 8:31-38

Then he began to teach them that the Son of Man must undergo great suffering, and be rejected by the elders, the chief priests, and the scribes, and be killed, and after three days rise again. He said all this quite openly. And Peter took him aside and began to rebuke him. But turning and looking at his disciples, he rebuked Peter and said, "Get behind me, Satan! For you are setting your mind not on divine things but on human things." He called the crowd with his disciples, and said to them, "If any want to become my followers, let them deny themselves and take up their cross and follow me. For those who want to save their life will lose it, and those who lose their life for my sake, and for the sake of the gospel, will save it. For what will it profit them to gain the whole world and forfeit their life? Indeed, what can they give in return for their life? Those who are ashamed of me and of my words in this adulterous and sinful generation, of them the Son of Man will also be ashamed when he comes in the glory of his Father with the holy angels."

The Bethsaida Boys

After Jesus was baptized by John, he went to spend time in the desert lands east of the Jordan River, to begin preparing for the work he was going to do. While he was there in the wilderness, he got word that John had been arrested and killed. It was then that he decided it was time to come back to Galilee and get to work.

He traveled around Galilee, which is not a big place, and began preaching and teaching, picking up where John the Baptist had stopped. We could spend a lot of time talking about John's relationship with Jesus or debating about the meaning of the things John had said about Jesus when he baptized him. We could also spend time analyzing the words we hear in the reading today; they were some pretty strong words at times. We could debate about whether these words were actually spoken by Jesus, or as some say, were added later by the early church to stress the importance of becoming a follower of the founder of their new "Christian" movement. We could spend time on those issues of faith. But I'd rather just remember the story, and see if it will tell me anything meaningful.

Bethsaida is a village in the northeastern corner of the Sea of Galilee. It's in a rich part of the land, with lots of orchards and vineyards, good farmland with strong crops. But the primary industry of Bethsaida, and the part that made it such a center for business, was fishing. The Sea of Galilee was filled with fish of all kinds, and Bethsaida was the number one fishing location around the entire rest of the sea. Fishing was big business in Bethsaida, and the people who ran those businesses weren't that much different from a business owner today. They spent a good part of their day doing routine business things — repairing their fleets of boats and fishing nets, making deals with the buyers who came down to the docks to purchase fish, and dealing with all of the things involved in managing employees, just keeping the business going. One of the larger fishing companies was run by a couple of brothers, and another by a fairly well-off gentleman who also had family living nearby in the town of Capernaum just a few miles along the shore to the west.

The story began on a fairly typical morning in Bethsaida. The warm breeze was blowing in to shore from the water, the gulls were screaming overhead looking for scraps, and the two brothers were there at the boat docks helping their crews mend nets and sort through the fish that had been caught the night before. A lot of fishing was done at night on the sea because they could hang lanterns on the side of the boat that drew the fish to the surface, making them easier to catch. These guys had studied their craft and knew all of the tricks. The brothers both had families. We don't know much more about them but it's clear they were hard workers, well established in their community and business, and were highly responsible members of the community. They were capable managers, strong, dependable, solid citizens.

The other fisherman, the one with family from Capernaum, was still out with his boats along with one of his brothers, trying to get a few more pounds of fish for the day's market. They were hard at work throwing their long nets from the boats, then slowly rowing in a circle and pulling the nets back in filled with fish. At some point a small group of people walked up along the shore. The strangers stopped and watched the fishermen at work for a while. Apparently, the fishing boat wasn't very far from land because at one point one of the guys in the group watching from shore yelled something to the fishermen. Now, we're not sure whether Simon or his brother Andrew even knew who Jesus was at this point, or if he would have recognized him when he saw him, or have recognized his voice when he hollered at them. All we know is that when Jesus yelled out to the two brothers, "Follow me," they pulled their boat to shore. I try to imagine the look on the faces of the other fishermen in the boat — the employees, as the two highly successful, highly responsible business owners dropped their nets in the boats and walked off down the shore with the group. I try to imagine what those fishermen must have thought as they stood there holding the boats, wondering if they still had jobs, whether they should go back out and catch more fish, or just go back to the boat dock and wait.

The story now moves to the boat dock in Bethsaida, where the brothers James and John were still hard at work. It apparently wasn't that much longer before the group arrived in Bethsaida and appeared at the docks, where the guys were hard at work mending a net in one of their boats. We don't hear just what Jesus said to the two brothers but we are simply told that they immediately got up from their boat, walked off of the boat dock that belonged to the company they owned — and for which they were responsible — and walked off down the shore with Jesus and the others.

Did I mention that James and John's father, Zebedee, was there in the boat, helping them mend the nets that morning? That really makes me wonder what was going through old Zebedee's mind. As we're told in the story, the fishermen didn't even make a quick detour by the office to let the secretary know what was happening. Even more, they apparently didn't even run by the house to say "so long" to their wives and kids, leave a forwarding address, or anything. All of that was apparently left for Zebedee to take care of. I'm guessing that Zebedee was probably the one who actually started the fishing business years ago when he was younger, building it from one boat to the fleet that was now tied to the boat dock. He probably had the dream that one day his two boys, James and John, would grow up and take over from him and build on his dream; that they would keep the family tradition going for their sons, and their sons, and so on. What was going through his mind as he sat there in the boat, holding a still unmended net, watching the two boys wander off down the shore, leaving him to take care of things here?

There's a chance that what really happened was a bit different. Maybe, when Jesus asked them to follow and they made the decision to do that, they took the time to put their affairs in order, helped their family understand what was happening, and did everything they could to make sure everyone and everything was going to be okay while they were gone. It would certainly be nice to think that they took that step. But, honestly, if we look at what was to follow with these guys, and some of the challenges Jesus faced with them, it just may well be that they did just what the story says and simply walked away. These were good men who had been responsible enough to run their businesses, but we're going to see that they all had their weaknesses. They could be stubborn at times and were more like us than the image of perfect disciples we sometimes create in our minds.

We're told they left Bethsaida and walked along the sea for just a couple of miles, until they got to Capernaum, where they stopped. They stayed long enough to visit the Capernaum synagogue, where we are told Jesus astounded everyone with his teaching. In fact, we find that for a large part of Jesus' ministry in Galilee over the next couple of years they were based out of Capernaum. Why? Remember that Simon Peter's family lived in Capernaum. They had a pretty good-sized home there, large enough at one point that we're told as many as forty or fifty people may have lived there, as they followed and listened to Jesus. Peter was one of those guys who was very quick to act, frequently before taking time to think. Many times Peter was one of those guys who seemed only to open his mouth long enough to change feet. As you may remember, later in the story we're told that Jesus decided to change Simon's name to Peter, after the word used for *rock*, because Peter was so strong in his views. Unfortunately, his strong views weren't always the wisest ones.

In my imagination, they were walking along the shore and someone asked Jesus where they were all going to stay for the night. Simon jumped in and said, "We can stay at my family's place in Capernaum!" It may be that Jesus had that in mind, but I think it's probably safe to say that it was Simon Peter's idea. Imagine the looks on the faces of Peter's family as he showed up at the door with this interesting group of people, letting Mom know there would be an extra dozen or so for dinner. Keep in mind that at least four of these guys were fishermen who had just walked away from their boats after a long night of fishing. There had been no shower, no change of clothes, nothing. I'm thinking they probably made quite an impression.

Fortunately, first-century custom was well-known for welcoming visitors and going out of the way to be hospitable to guests for three days. According to custom, guests were welcome in the home for three days, after which they needed to move along and find a new place to rest their weary heads. So, can you see the look in the eyes around the table as Simon Peter mentions in passing that his friends plan on staying and making this home for a while? This was Peter's family and they must have known him well, so perhaps they were prepared for another one of his surprises like this — perhaps. I wonder if they were also ready for some of the things that would happen while they lived there, like the day the house was so full of visitors that a group of people actually ripped a hole in the roof to lower a sick man into the room so Jesus could heal him? Or the day the group of priests showed up at the door trying to start an argument with Jesus and nearly started a riot in town? Let's continue with the story, but just keep in mind that we really need to keep an eye on Simon Peter and be prepared for whatever he might do next.

Let's not single out Simon Peter and make it sound like he was some kind of a problem disciple. As the story is told, every one of the disciples turned out to be what you might call a challenge. Mark's version of the story gives us some good examples.

Remember the day a bunch of them came running up to Jesus saying, "We found someone over there who was casting out demons and helping people, and he was doing it in your name. So we made him cut it out and move on down the road!" Jesus probably took a deep breath before he said, "Guys, remember that anyone who is not out there actively working against us, is actually *for* us. So leave the guy alone!"

Another time Jesus walked up to a group of people who were angry and yelling at some of the disciples, and when he asked about it one of the people said, "My son is very sick and your disciples said they could cast out the demon that was hurting him. But they couldn't do it!" Again, I see Jesus taking a deep breath and shaking his head before saying, "How long do I have to put up with you guys?"

Think about the day they were walking back to Capernaum and Jesus heard the disciples arguing among themselves. He asked them what the problem was and they told him, "We're trying to figure out which one of us is the greatest disciple and gets to sit next to you when you teach." Can you get an idea of the look on Jesus' face this time?

Jesus praised a man for giving away his riches to demonstrate his commitment to helping the poor, and Peter jumped up and said, "Lord, what about us? We have left everything and followed you!" Jesus responded by saying, "Yes, but many of those who are first will end up last, and those who are last will end up first." The look on Peter's face and the group's general grumbling about that statement had to have had Jesus shaking his head as well.

It's not that the disciples were ignorant, selfish, or bad guys. But keep in mind who they really were. We know that at least four of them were former business leaders. Another of them was a tax collector who had to have the same business savvy as the CEO of a fishing company. Another member of the group was a political hothead, a Zealot. These were all guys who were used to making decisions, were used to leading things, and had all been at least relatively successful in what they did. They knew how to lead, how to build an organization, and they knew how to deal with competitors. Becoming a disciple did not remove any of that and did not somehow magically make them wiser or holier. Becoming a disciple simply challenged them to learn how to use their strengths in very different ways — and it was clearly a very slow process. In fact, it wasn't until after Jesus was gone that Peter was finally able to put his strengths to good use, when he stood up in the middle of the crowded streets and began to preach about what Jesus had actually done. The old saying is "better late than never," but at least he finally got it!

For almost three years, these disciples traveled around with Jesus, watching, listening, and trying to figure out what it meant to be people of faith. Essentially, they had to learn how to reverse most of what they had come to believe about success and about winning. As business leaders or zealots, they believed in winning and in overcoming any obstacle that got in the way of being successful and growing their business. That's the kind of person Jesus needed in his group of disciples, people with that kind of passion for winning. But they needed to redefine just what winning actually meant, and this is where all the problems arose.

To the disciples, winning meant becoming more powerful and rich, more secure and forcing your way to the top of the heap. Jesus talked about winning and success as becoming poor, taking risks, and being willing to give up all normal securities. The poor and meek would be the real winners. Those who were first would actually end up being last, and the last would be in first place. For a long time, the disciples tried very hard to educate this well-meaning, but clearly inexperienced preacher, honestly trying to help him understand the flaws in his approach. In my imagination, I can see many evenings sitting around the fire while the disciples lectured Jesus on good business and marketing principles, trying to help him understand. You build on strengths, not weaknesses. You confront competition with force, not with meekness. They were trying to be helpful.

After three years, Jesus' popularity and visibility had grown to a point at which he was recognized wherever he went. He was becoming more of a high-profile target and it was clear that the final confrontation with the religious leaders and others was drawing near. Unfortunately, it was also clear to Jesus that his disciples just weren't ready for it; they were still not at all clear about what was going to happen and why. As he did at the beginning of his ministry, Jesus went into the wilderness for a time of reflection and preparation for what was about to come. This time he took the disciples with him and traveled to Caesarea Philippi, a place far to the north where he would not be well known and could make one more attempt to help the disciples prepare. Caesarea Philippi was actually a pretty fancy vacation spot, a resort for the Romans and others. It was most certainly not a place a faithful Jewish person would even pass through, let alone where he would spend time.

The disciples, all good boys from good Jewish families, were probably horrified that he brought them there, and it was during one of the heated conversations one evening that Jesus took over the conversation by saying, "Back in Bethsaida, where all of the crowds are coming to see me, who do the people say that I am?" They all spoke up with a variety of responses, but he quickly continued, "And, who do *you* say that I am?" (v. 29).

Seeing it as a perfect opportunity to highlight the potential for the ministry if Jesus would just listen to common sense, the story tells us they used words like "Lord." Mark tells us that Peter said Jesus was the messiah, the new leader of the true faith. Even for Peter, that's a huge claim. When folks used the term messiah at that time, they envisioned the person sent from God who would come and reclaim the leadership of the faith and of the nation. The enemies would be thrown out, the temple would be cleansed, and an entirely new way of life would be put in place. The messiah Peter was referring to was the ultimate winner, the top of the heap, the one to make everything eternally secure.

Jesus responded, once again, by trying to help redefine things for Peter. He said that what was actually coming was a time of tremendous suffering that would lead to Jesus being killed. We're told that it was all finally just too much for Peter, and he pulled Jesus aside from the group to rebuke him, to get him to understand once and for all that this kind of negative talk was not the way to become successful. I would love to have seen the look on Peter's face as Jesus turned away from him, saying "Get behind me Satan!" (v. 33) saying that he was focusing on the wrong things, focusing on human rather than divine things. He was focusing on the wrong definition of success. As Jesus turned back to the rest of the group, was Peter angry, was he confused, or did he finally begin to understand? Based on the fact that in just a few days he would end up denying that he even knew Jesus, it doesn't seem that he did understand.

Calling one of his own disciples "Satan" probably shook up the entire group for a few minutes, so Jesus used that opportunity to try and help them understand. He explained once again that those who would be his followers would deny themselves, take up their crosses and follow him. Those three things would have meant something a bit different to them than it does for us listening now.

Denying themselves simply meant to stop trusting in some human level of success and to trust that if you focus on being faithful, doing the things that real faith in God challenges you to do, you will end up winning. Becoming a major power and smashing all opposition is not the goal. Instead, seeing that the hungry are fed, the naked clothed, and the hopeless hope-filled; all make it possible for the last to become first. In other words, we need to redefine success.

Taking up their crosses was not some kind of a theological or philosophical concept for these guys. As they have traveled around the countryside over the past three years, the image of carrying a cross had been burned into their psyche. Crucifixion was a popular tool the Romans used at that time because it served two purposes. It got rid of individuals who caused trouble for the empire, and it made a really big impression on everyone else. That's because crucifixions were typically done along the roadside by nailing a crossbar to a tree and then nailing the victim to the crossbar. Writings from this period describe traveling a hundred miles along a road, seeing so many crucifixions that each crossbar actually touched the next, mile after mile. It was clear to the disciples what Jesus meant, and it was not at all in line with how they would think of a successful end to this venture. It had to have grown very quiet at this point.

Clearly they were beginning to understand just how different an experience this was going to end up being. If this visit to Caesarea Philippi was intended to get them thinking seriously about the future, that goal was met. The story continued as Jesus led the group south to Jerusalem, and while the boys still occasionally struggled with the roles they were to play, especially poor Peter, they had begun to understand what it meant to actually follow this Jesus of Galilee.

As we come to the end of this part of the story, think just how hard it must have been for the disciples to figure Jesus out and get it right. Think about all of the times they totally screwed it up, and yet in the end, had the impact that they had. It makes me feel more and more comfortable that, somehow, God will find a way to use us too. That's good news.

Lent 3
John 2:13-22

The Passover of the Jews was near, and Jesus went up to Jerusalem. In the temple he found people selling cattle, sheep, and doves, and the money changers seated at their tables. Making a whip of cords, he drove all of them out of the temple, both the sheep and the cattle. He also poured out the coins of the money changers and overturned their tables. He told those who were selling the doves, "Take these things out of here! Stop making my Father's house a marketplace!" His disciples remembered that it was written, "Zeal for your house will consume me." The Jews then said to him, "What sign can you show us for doing this?" Jesus answered them, "Destroy this temple, and in three days I will raise it up." The Jews then said, "This temple has been under construction for forty-six years, and will you raise it up in three days?" But he was speaking of the temple of his body. After he was raised from the dead, his disciples remembered that he had said this; and they believed the scripture and the word that Jesus had spoken.

Zeal!

Have you ever had one of those times when you had just had enough? One of those times that you have held your breath, you have turned away, maybe many times, because you just don't like what you see going on, but then finally come to the point that you just can't turn away one more time? You've had enough, and you decide you just can't be silent any longer. So you do something fairly dramatic. Looking back on it, it may not have been all that smart, but you had had enough and you did it. Can you remember one of those times? Take just a moment and search your memory, and maybe this story about Jesus cleansing the temple will make a little more sense.

But before we actually begin the story let's recognize some of the confusion around this incident and get it out of the way so we can hear what the story actually has to say to us. Sometimes we get distracted by things and miss out on what the story is actually trying to tell us.

Today's version of the story from John's gospel takes place at the beginning of Jesus' ministry, during his first visit to Jerusalem for Passover. John tells us that Jesus actually made at least three trips to Jerusalem for the Passover. The other gospel writers only tell us about Jesus making one trip to Jerusalem for Passover — at the end of his three years of ministry. It was during that visit when Jesus entered the city on a donkey in the big parade and walked into the temple where our story takes place. John tells the story differently. Does it matter? Let's hear the story one more time together and you can decide if it really makes any difference.

It was Passover. Passover is one of the largest holidays of the Jewish faith, remembering and celebrating the Exodus of the slaves out of Egypt with Moses, centuries earlier. Every faithful Jew who was capable was supposed to travel to Jerusalem and present an offering at the temple. By presenting their offering they not only received forgiveness for all of their sins but they were also demonstrating their loyal obedience as a faithful Jew. So Jews traveled from all over the world to be at the temple on Passover, and that included Jesus and his followers, who came to town with all of the other faithful Galileans prepared to make their sacrificial offering.

Try to imagine what the Passover experience was like. The typically busy city was now stretched to the limit with visitors from all around the world, wearing all manner of colorful clothing, and speaking dozens of different languages. Rooms were full, streets were packed, and everyone was focused on one thing: getting to the crowded temple to offer their Passover sacrifice.

While Passover meant a time for families to get together for huge feasts and celebrations, the center of the holiday was the moment they went to the temple and offered their required sacrifice to the temple priests. It had been a practice since the time of Moses, one that continued in the temple of David's time, and in Jesus' generation in the temple high on the hill overlooking the city.

The specific type of sacrifice you had to make depended on many things: where you were from, how old you were, what your job was, how nasty the sins were for which you needed to be forgiven, and a long list of other things. Your sacrifice might be as simple as a dove and a half bushel of wheat, or something more elaborate like a full-sized, unblemished oxen. Most sacrifices included at least some form of animal, and the requirement was that the animal be perfect and free of blemish. This not only meant it should be physically perfect but it needed to be clean and look nice and healthy as well.

This leads to an interesting issue for those coming from out of town. Can you imagine the challenge of traveling a good distance across country, mostly by walking the crowded and narrow roads, typically for many days, and the entire time dragging along a few crates of doves, several bushel of grain, not to mention a couple of sheep or oxen? You not only needed to keep the animals from wandering off and getting injured from the hours of walking on the rocky paths, but you needed to bring enough food for them so they looked nice, fat, and healthy when you finally got them through the crowds, up the steps, and into the temple. You needed to keep them clean as well.

It's not surprising that most travelers thought it was best to not bring their sacrificial animals with them, but to wait and buy them once they got to Jerusalem. As a result, there was quite a variety of vendors set up in their booths around the temple yards, all offering the types of sacrifice that travelers needed to purchase. Because the visitors had to purchase their sacrifice there, the vendors were able to charge more, kind of like buying gasoline along the interstate instead of driving a few extra miles where you can find better prices. It was truly a seller's market.

Just making sense of all of those rules was nearly impossible for most folks as well, so what you actually had to sacrifice depended a lot upon who you knew and asked. As an example, one of the things people argued about was what you did with the sacrificial animal that you purchased, after you purchased it. Some said that you could just get it from the vendor and take it to the priests. Others argued that if you touched the animal yourself, it became unclean, so the only option was to have one of the temple workers take your animal from the vendor to the priest, which would be done for a small fee. One of the religious rule books of the day describes that argument:

> "Jose ben Joezer says: On a festival day a man may not lay his hands on the offering before it is slaughtered. Joseph ben Johanan says he may. Joshua b. Perahyah says he may not. Nittai the Arbelite says he may. Judah b. Tabbai says he may not. Simeon b. Shetah says he may. Shemaiah says he may. Abtalion says he may not. Shammai says he may not lay on his hands. Hillel says he may" (Hagigah 2.2). Every rabbi interpreted the rules in their own way, so what you had to do and pay depended on just how well you knew how to play the game.

In addition, every person entering the temple courtyard itself was required to pay an admission fee of one-half shekel of Tyre, which was a fairly common coin in Jerusalem at that time. However those coming from out of town were probably carrying money from their home location, which more than likely meant they did not have one-half shekel of Tyre. So before entering the temple to offer their sacrifice, they had to visit one of the many moneychangers who were scattered among the vendors, and who were known to charge whatever exchange rate they could get from those needing their services.

But there was more. The way the process worked was that you would take your sacrifice to the temple courtyard where it would be presented to one of the priests. Sacrificial animals were killed and butchered, parts of the animal were burned on the altar fire as the law required, and the rest of the meat was thrown into a large pot and cooked, to be used as part of the various Passover feasts. This is important to remember because according to law, the priests would throw the meat into the boiling pot and let the meat cook for a while. After the meat had cooked up and begun to fall apart, the priest would take a huge fork and jab it down into the pot and when he pulled it back up, any of the meat that was stuck to the fork would be given to the priests for their own food, as a part of their salary. However if we stand here and watch people take their animals up to the priests, we see them butcher the animal and throw scraps in the fire and drop the rest of the meat over into the boiling pot. But the priest waits perhaps thirty seconds, then takes that big fork and jabs it down into the pot. When he pulls it up he's got an entire side of meat that takes two hands to pull out of the pot.

So get the picture. Noise, crowds of people needing to buy a sacrifice, going from vendor to vendor who are all yelling about their pricing. The animals are running everywhere, and there are the sounds and the smells that come with having animals running around all over the place. You have moneychangers and people arguing and bickering over exchange rates. You watch the people paying to enter the courtyard and humbly presenting their sacrifice to the priests, and watch as their "holy" sacrifice is quickly turned into just another revenue stream for those who are running the show.

Anyone who became upset about what they saw and who went to the authorities to complain were sent to the Sadducees, who oversaw the operations of the temple. Keep in mind that the Sadducees were the rich folks who lived in the big homes near the temple. They received a percentage of the income from the sacrificial vendors, the moneychangers, and the priests. Let's just say that they weren't all that sympathetic to those disapproving of the business dealings taking place during Passover.

That feels a little irritating to you standing and watching this, so it might help explain what went through Jesus' mind as he stepped up the stairs, entered the temple courtyard, and stood there watching and listening. Then he came to that moment when he had finally had enough. We're told he grabbed some rope from one of the vendor tents and started swinging it around like a whip, chasing vendors, moneychangers, and livestock out of the temple courtyard. He grabbed the metal

51

boxes the moneychangers used to hold their loot and poured the coins out all over the ground, which had to have created a stir all by itself. As he did this, he was shouting: "Take these things out of here!" and "Stop making my Father's house a marketplace!"

Let's pause right there for just a moment to point out that Jesus was not yelling at us and telling us that we can't have bake sales or fall festivals in the church. His anger was not about the fact that something was being sold but that those doing the selling were taking complete advantage of those buying. It wasn't that money was involved; it was that one group was treating the other as if they were worthless and had no value in the eyes of God. They were doing that in the very place that was meant to be the ultimate symbol of fairness and equality among all people, God's temple. So, he drew a line. He took a stand.

It got a lot of attention. But while we let Jesus go ahead and finish his house cleaning, we might look around the rest of the temple courtyard.

Over there were those Sadducees with the money and the power, watching this man cutting into their income stream, something they clearly could not allow to continue. Standing next to them were the priests, wearing their robes symbolizing their holiness and power, watching this naïve preacher from Galilee make them look like a bunch of crooks. Did I mention the Romans? We can't forget the Romans.

During Jesus' lifetime, the temple in Jerusalem is the second largest building in the city. The largest building is actually right next door to the temple, standing just a couple of meters higher, just to make a point. This is the Antonia Fortress, built by the Romans to hold squads of soldiers. Their sole purpose was to make sure that nothing ever happened in Jerusalem that might become a problem. King Herod was the current overseer of the land, and the way he kept his job was to make sure that Rome never confronted a problem in

Jerusalem. Herod was crazy, but he was also cautious, so during the Passover holiday we're told he had a Roman centurion standing at every pillar in the temple area, and another squad standing at the top of the Antonia Fortress, watching, just to make sure there was never any problem. I think we can be sure they were all watching Jesus quite closely.

In the game of chess, it is often said that there are actually three different games being played: the opening, the middle game, and the end game. In the opening game, the players begin positioning their pieces on the board in a way that will allow them to do something meaningful later. In the middle game, the players use a range of strategies to create power and build their strength. In the end game, the players rely upon all that has been done so far and watch for the moment to make their final attack to win the game. There is no turning back from the end game.

Jesus has begun his end game today in the temple. It may well be that Mark is more accurate in telling us this story took place during Jesus' final visit to the city, because it seems highly unlikely that any of the powers-that-be would have been open to allowing him to go back home and stir things up for another three years. Even the disciples realized it. As they watched him, one of them said that it reminded him of Psalm 69, in which the writer spoke to God and said: "Zeal for your house will consume me!" (v. 17). Although the disciples weren't always that bright, they clearly understood that what Jesus was doing was going to end up consuming him. They might not have understood everything that was to come, but they realized he had had enough, and he wasn't going to sit back any longer. Enough was enough. The end game had begun.

Let's end our retelling of this story with a couple of important points. First, as suggested earlier, Jesus wasn't making a point about bake sales and fall festivals, though I've heard some amazing arguments against them based on this story. He was upset that one person was not treating another person as an equal, as another child of God.

Second, the story is not a call for all of us to become zealous about some issue and to go out and turn over tables and drive away the evildoers. We live in a time that is running wild with zealots, each proclaiming their view of right and doing horrendous things to other human beings, far beyond turning over tables and swinging a rope. No one can take this story of Jesus in the temple and use it to justify an act of abuse or terror of any kind — no one. We don't see the world as the Son of God sees the world, so any zealous act we might pursue is going to be corrupted through our limited understanding.

What might we take from this story, other than understanding a bit more about why Jesus did what he did that day in the temple? The story's message seems clear. Our task is to zealously make sure that our church, this house of God, never becomes a place in which any one person is treated as less equal to, or less valuable than, any other person. Our task is to keep the house clean of those things that might cause any person to feel less at home here, less safe here, or less welcome here.

Our task is to obey the one rule of the clean house: "This one commandment I give to you: love one another."

Lent 4
John 3:14-21

And just as Moses lifted up the serpent in the wilderness, so must the Son of Man be lifted up, that whoever believes in him may have eternal life. "For God so loved the world that he gave his only Son, so that everyone who believes in him may not perish but may have eternal life. Indeed, God did not send the Son into the world to condemn the world, but in order that the world might be saved through him. Those who believe in him are not condemned; but those who do not believe are condemned already, because they have not believed in the name of the only Son of God. And this is the judgment, that the light has come into the world, and people loved darkness rather than light because their deeds were evil. For all who do evil hate the light and do not come to the light, so that their deeds may not be exposed. But those who do what is true come to the light, so that it may be clearly seen that their deeds have been done in God."

Rebirth

The city of Jerusalem was packed with strangers during the Passover feast, so you could walk a long distance and never see anyone you recognized. He was counting on that, as he quickly moved along the streets with his head held low and his face covered. He moved from alleyway to alleyway, looking carefully in all directions before stepping into the openness of a street, making sure there was not someone who might recognize him. But while he tried to remain hidden, he had to be careful to not appear too suspicious and cause someone to think he might be a criminal. With the huge crowds in town for the festival, the centurions and other officials were on guard and watching closely for thieves and pickpockets hiding in the shadows. Even though he could quickly clear up any problem by showing them who he was, having to do that would create even bigger problems. So he had to be careful.

This story in today's scripture raises a lot of questions for many people. At one point, Jesus says that God loved the world so much that he sent his only Son to save it, and then turns around and says that those people who do not believe in him will be condemned. We need to look at the full story, and learn what was actually going on, to see if that helps us make sense out of those things John tells us that Jesus said.

But before we listen to the story again, it might be helpful if we take a few minutes to remember how and why these stories were written. It might help us understand why there sometimes seem to be these confusing passages in the four gospels, and might help us hear the stories more clearly as they were intended to be heard.

Mark was the first "Jesus book" written, probably around 60 CE, some thirty years after the stories took place. It is brief, to the point, and tells the story of Jesus in a step-by-step process and in a very simple language. Originally it ended at chapter 16:8 when Mary ran from the tomb after the angel told her Jesus had been raised and that the disciples should go to meet him in Galilee. The rest of chapter 16 is written in a different style and language, added in perhaps the second or even fourth century.

Matthew was written sometime around 80 CE, after the destruction of Jerusalem by the Romans in 70 CE. The author was very familiar with Judaism and kept a clear focus on Jewish history and the law. It's interesting to remember that the original writings had no chapters or verses or punctuation. To make it a bit more clear, Matthew divided his book into five major discourses, or sections, perhaps to compare to the five books of the Jewish Torah, called the Pentateuch. Matthew was most likely writing his book for Jewish readers, in an attempt to help them understand who Jesus was.

Luke was the storyteller. He borrowed a lot from the writings of Mark, much of it copied word for word. It was written perhaps around 85 CE, in a style used by the Greeks, suggesting that the goal was to present the story of Jesus to Gentile readers. Instead of focusing on the law, Luke wrote to present a theological argument to his readers. It tells much the same story as the other gospels, but in a more structured and logical manner, with an emphasis on Jesus' compassion rather than a focus on the law like Matthew. Luke uses lots of colorful stories to paint a powerful picture of what Jesus did and who he was.

John was probably written sometime around 90 CE, in Ephesus in modern Turkey. The new Christian group was under increasing persecution by both the Romans and the

Jews, so it was becoming extremely dangerous to be a Christian. While this book tells many of the same stories as the other gospels, John changes the order of many of the stories, and changes some of the details of stories as well. But it's important to remember that John is not writing to simply retell stories but to make it very clear that a battle is taking place. Matthew, Mark, and Luke typically refer to Jesus as a *teacher*, *preacher*, and sometimes as a *Son of God*. John pulls no punches and describes him as *Lord* and *Messiah*, making it clear that what is actually going on is a full battle that will end in life or death. John writes in colorful language for the Greeks and Romans, using concepts like bread, water, shepherds, doors, light, and darkness. But his goal is to shine light on the freedom and the new life that comes from following Jesus' commandment to love one another.

As we look at these books we call the gospels, we find that Mark is the first version, focusing on the basic and simple facts, told in a way that was easy to remember and retell, almost like an early news story about what has happened.

Matthew probably wrote next, directly addressing his stories to the Jewish readers as the early church was just beginning to take shape.

As the church began to grow, and the disciples moved around to avoid persecution, Luke was written in a Greek or Roman land, to introduce Jesus to people who did not know Jewish history or law, but were highly religious in other ways.

John wrote to that same very logical Gentile audience, but at a time when the early church was really beginning to feel the pressures of persecution. In John's community there were more and more attempts to discredit Christianity and argue that Jesus was merely a good preacher who ended up being killed. John's goal was to change the minds of his enemies.

Remember that our story today is being told by John, and at least part of the message the storyteller wants us to hear is that there is a battle taking place, for our very lives. Let's hear the story again.

The city of Jerusalem was packed with strangers during the Passover feast, so you could walk a long distance and never see anyone you recognized. Jesus' mysterious visitor was counting on that, as he quickly moved along the streets with this head held low and his face covered. He moved from alleyway to alleyway, looking carefully in all directions before stepping into the openness of a street, making sure there was not someone there who might recognize him.

Finally, he came to the end of his search, walked up to a certain house, and knocked on the door. We're not told who answered the door but we can be certain that whoever it was, the expression on their face when they saw the visitor would have been the same look of amazement, mixed with pure terror. Even without his robes, they would have recognized this man, a Pharisee. More than that, this man was one of the key leaders of the community, a member of the Sanhedrin itself. The Sanhedrin was an exclusive group of 23 men who made up the official religious court of the Jewish faith in Jerusalem. They were the judges of the faith with powers that no other Jewish court had, and with such tight connections with the temple that their court building, called the Hall of Hewn Stones, was built into the side of the temple mount itself. Whoever it was, this is probably what went through their mind during that first fraction of a second after they opened the door and recognized Nicodemus standing there:

> It was the Pharisees who opposed John the Baptist and ended up getting him arrested and killed. Then they were after Jesus. After all, he went into their temple and tore things up. He argued with them in front of everyone, called them names and made them look really bad. Because of that, many people ended up turning away from the Pharisees and following him. Jesus

had become so popular there was no way they could arrest him publicly without causing a riot. So here they were, coming at night to take him away and shut him up.

We can only imagine what happened in the next few minutes, but based on other stories we have about the disciples, it probably went something like this: The disciple at the door told Nicodemus to wait and went inside to tell another disciple and figure out what they should do. They ended up telling a couple of others, and they quickly ended up in a full-blown panic, arguing about the best way to get Jesus out of the house and make a run for Galilee where they might be safe. At some point Jesus heard the noise, asked what was going on, and was told about Nicodemus standing out in the street. Jesus looked at them calmly, probably shook his head a bit, and told them to let him in.

Can you picture what took place after that? There is Jesus sitting on a mat on the floor, and sitting on a mat next to him is one of the top religious leaders of the nation, one of the most powerful men in the country. We'll just ignore all of the disciples standing around the edges watching: Peter trying to figure out the quickest escape route from the house and Judas keeping one hand on the sword he has tucked under his tunic. Instead, we'll focus on the conversation between the two men sitting on the floor.

John tells us that Nicodemus started the conversation with "Rabbi, we know that you are a teacher who has come from God..." (v. 2). These are great setup words, spoken to sound like you are paying someone a compliment to get them off-guard just before you move in for the kill. When Nicodemus said these words, I can see Peter rolling his eyes and mumbling to Judas, "Okay, here it comes." But instead of using his authority as a leader of the Jewish faith to attack Jesus, Nicodemus' voice lowered a bit, and even seemed to take on the sound of true respect, as he said: "I tell you, no one can do the things you do apart from the presence of God" (v. 2).

Peter and the others were completely confused and began looking around at each other hoping someone could make sense of what was going on. Instead of attacking Jesus, Nicodemus was talking to him as a student talks with a teacher. It slowly began to dawn on them that Nicodemus hadn't come here in the middle of the night to hide from the crowds and arrest Jesus, but he had come at night to hide from his fellow Pharisees in order to ask questions that no good Pharisee would ask, especially not a member of the Sanhedrin. Nicodemus was trying to understand.

Jesus then spoke and told Nicodemus the reason he was having a hard time understanding what Jesus was doing, saying: "Very truly I say to you, no one can see the kingdom of God without being born from above" (v. 3). I would love to see the look on Nicodemus' face. You see, Nicodemus was a logical man. His entire life as a Pharisee and member of the Sanhedrin was based on interpreting the stacks of books filled with religious laws and making decisions that impacted people's lives. Nicodemus was used to dealing in facts, in concrete matters, interpreting laws to make decisions between black and white, good and evil, right and wrong. So we need to feel some sympathy for him as he looked back at Jesus and asked, "How can anyone be born after having grown old? Can one enter a second time into the mother's womb and be born?" (v. 4).

To Nicodemus, being born again meant exactly that: being physically born again. He wasn't trying to argue or disagree with Jesus, he was just completely lost and befuddled, with some pretty ludicrous images going through his mind as he tried to make sense of it all.

This is where our piece of scripture picks up the story today. It is as if we're standing against the wall in that room listening to the conversation as Jesus tried to help Nicodemus understand.

Over the next few minutes, Jesus explained that he wasn't talking about another physical birth, but something else, a birth that occurred in the spirit, a birth that changed what was inside the person more than what was outside. He told Nicodemus that the way to have this second birth was to believe in what Jesus was saying about God, that God loved the world so much that he sent his own Son to deliver the message and to give his life to make sure it was understood.

He explained the idea of being born again using terms that Nicodemus would clearly understand, by comparing what he was offering with what Nicodemus and the Sanhedrin were offering. He said that God's goal was not to condemn the world, not to hold some holy session of court, find people guilty of things, and condemn them to some eternal punishment. They already had that. There were so many religious laws that it was impossible for anyone to follow them all, which meant that everyone was already condemned. What Jesus was offering was an opportunity to start a new life in which no one was doomed to be condemned. Jesus explained that God saw every person as having value, loved as much as every other person. Jesus was offering light to replace the darkness of the old way.

We're not told what went through Nicodemus' mind or how the conversation ended. John immediately takes us back to Galilee for more stories.

In my imagination, I watch Nicodemus as he sat there listening to the things Jesus was saying. I suspect he was almost in shock, as he slowly began to understand the truth of what Jesus was telling him. He had lived his entire life studying and enforcing laws and knew it was true that no person could ever follow them all, not even himself. And if the truth was known, every person, even those Sanhedrin members themselves, would be found guilty of breaking religious laws and would be condemned. He knew that the only reason this did not happen was that they hid their sins, they covered them in darkness and pretended that they did not exist. They lived a life that was not true, a life that was just an act, constantly in fear of someone shining a light into their dark places and revealing who they really were. If a person could truly believe that God loved them regardless of their mistakes, instead of condemning them, that would truly be like being born a second time. And at that moment, something began to change inside Nicodemus. Some spark of a new hope, a new life, as if he actually was born again.

Being born again is sometimes a difficult concept today and it has many interpretations. Too often, we end up creating rules and laws about what it means to be born again. We create tests for people to pass in order to prove they are born again and we use it as a yardstick to judge someone's value to us. As a result, it turns out to be just another way of creating darkness in people's lives. That's not what being born again is all about. If we want to understand what Jesus meant when he said that a person needed to be born a second time, all we need to do is look at Nicodemus.

How do I know that? Although John ends this story and moves on, this is not the last time we see and hear from Nicodemus. During another visit to Jerusalem for the Feast of the Unleavened Bread, the temple police saw Jesus in the temple and ran to the authorities to come up with a plan to arrest him and see that he was silenced once and for all. One of those authorities was Nicodemus, and as the group plotted about how to trap Jesus, Nicodemus spoke up saying, "Our law does not judge people without first giving them a hearing to find out what they are doing, does it?" Although they all turned on him and called him names, the result was that Jesus was safe.

We see Nicodemus once more, this time in a very different role than as a religious authority. John tells us that after the crucifixion, two men found a tomb for Jesus' burial, purchased and carried one hundred pounds of oils and spices to the tomb, and wrapped the body to give it a proper burial. One of those men was Joseph of Arimathea. The other was Nicodemus.

According to tradition, Nicodemus ended up being killed as a martyr, by the very laws he had once lived for. Today there are religious holidays and churches named for him and he is considered a saint.

That, my friends, is what it means to be born again.

Lent 5
John 12:20-33

Now among those who went up to worship at the festival were some Greeks. They came to Philip, who was from Bethsaida in Galilee, and said to him, "Sir, we wish to see Jesus." Philip went and told Andrew; then Andrew and Philip went and told Jesus. Jesus answered them, "The hour has come for the Son of Man to be glorified. Very truly, I tell you, unless a grain of wheat falls into the earth and dies, it remains just a single grain; but if it dies, it bears much fruit. Those who love their life lose it, and those who hate their life in this world will keep it for eternal life. Whoever serves me must follow me, and where I am, there will my servant be also. Whoever serves me, the Father will honor. Now my soul is troubled. And what should I say — 'Father, save me from this hour'? No, it is for this reason that I have come to this hour. Father, glorify your name." Then a voice came from heaven, "I have glorified it, and I will glorify it again." The crowd standing there heard it and said that it was thunder. Others said, "An angel has spoken to him." Jesus answered, "This voice has come for your sake, not for mine. Now is the judgment of this world; now the ruler of this world will be driven out. And I, when I am lifted up from the earth, will draw all people to myself." He said this to indicate the kind of death he was to die.

Some Greeks

Jesus was back in Jerusalem for another Passover. According to John's gospel, this was the third time Jesus and the disciples attended the Passover festival and each time they were there they got in trouble. The first two times they somehow got out of town and made it back up north to Galilee to continue their ministry. It would be much more difficult to accomplish that this time. Everywhere Jesus went he drew a big crowd. People had heard about this teacher from Galilee, and the things he was saying. More importantly, they had heard about some of the miracles Jesus had performed, and people have always been more impressed with miracles and magic than with teaching, so anytime he was around they wanted to be there to see what he might do next.

For this visit, Jesus was staying with his friends in Bethany, the little town just on the other side of the Mount of Olives from Jerusalem. It was a risky place to stay if Jesus was trying to stay off the radar with the crowds and the leaders in Jerusalem. Bethany was the home of Lazarus, and it had been just a short time since Lazarus had died and Jesus had brought him back to life. That's the kind of miracle that draws a crowd. But apparently Jesus and the disciples had slipped into town unnoticed, and John tells us they had all gotten together for dinner with friends, including Lazarus.

If we can get the picture in our minds of what that dinner was like back then, it will help us make sense of what was about to happen. Let's begin by taking the legs off of the tables and placing the tabletops on the floor, in kind of a horseshoe formation or an upside down letter "u." Everyone sat around the outside of the table, leaving the inside space open for those serving the food. Take away the chairs. Everyone would have been lying on cushions around the table, everyone reclining on their left sides and leaning on their left arms, eating and drinking with their right hands, with their legs and feet extending out behind them, away from the table. This was the common way of eating a meal and most certainly how it was done during Passover. So we can picture Jesus reclining at the table, surrounded by the disciples and their friends, with Martha scurrying around serving the meal. There is a good chance there were others in the room as well, though we're not told about them. It was tradition that before a special meal was served, the door to the house would be opened and any poor or hungry be allowed to enter the room and stand around the walls behind the table. As the people at the table ate their meal, any scraps they did not want were thrown over their shoulders to the poor, who then gathered up the crumbs and had their meal as well.

It is helpful to understand one other thing as well. At some point during the meal, it was customary for one of the servants to take a bowl of water and wash the feet of each of the guests, drying them with a towel. It actually served two purposes. First, since everyone wore sandals and spent most of their time walking through the dirt and dust outside, it just made things a bit tidier with all of those feet sticking out around the table as everyone ate their meal. In addition, it was an act of kindness, intended to make the guests feel welcomed in the house, a sign of respect from the host whose servants did the washing.

While Mary was busy serving, one of the servants was making his way around the table with a bowl of water and towel, washing the feet of the guests. I don't know if she had thought about it and planned it, or if it just struck her at the moment and she reacted, but when the servant came to Jesus, Mary went over and took the servant's place. Instead of using the bowl of water, Mary took a small vial from around her neck and poured the expensive perfume from it onto Jesus' feet. Rather than use the dirty towel, she wiped off the oil using her own hair. As the aroma of the perfume spread through the room, it would have stopped any conversation taking place and every eye in the place would have been on either Mary or Jesus. Apparently Judas was the first to speak, accusing Mary of wasting the valuable perfume that might have been sold and the money given to the poor. Knowing Judas, he probably gave a sympathetic nod to those actual poor people standing around the walls just to make his point more dramatic. I wonder what was going through Mary's head at that point? Others would probably have picked up Judas' argument, and the glares from the wall standers were probably pretty intense as well. It was probably one of those rather tense moments. I wonder if she braced herself for a scolding from Jesus as well.

But Jesus understood something the others were too distracted to understand. He remembered that all Jewish women carried a vial of perfume on a cord around their neck, as expensive as they could afford. For many women, it was the most valuable item they ever owned. That small vial carried the perfumes that were used to anoint the dead, and they carried it to make sure that their family could give her the proper burial she should have as a good Jewish woman. In the heat of the moment, although the disciples had been with Jesus for three years, none of them understood the message that Mary understood.

How word got out that Jesus was in town we don't know. Perhaps it was one of the people standing around the walls during dinner that went home and told people, but the next morning the crowds had begun to gather after hearing that Jesus was in town. We're told that other big crowds came just to see Lazarus too. The authorities were just as intent on getting rid of Lazarus as they were of getting rid of Jesus.

Having a dead man come back to life was pretty hard to refute, and many people had left the temple to follow Jesus just because of Lazarus. Everyone came hoping to see more miracles, to have some proof, to know for certain that Jesus was the one who was going to turn everything around. As the crowds grew, things became more and more volatile. We're not really told what Jesus wanted to have happen that day, but as it began to unfold, it seems that things began to get out of control.

As Jesus began to walk up the hill toward Jerusalem, some in the group grabbed branches of palm trees and started waving them around in the air. This looks to us like a great celebration and something Jesus would appreciate. But again, it helps to understand a bit more about the situation. While it is true that we look at the palm branch as a symbol of peace, the odds are that was not the message the palm wavers were wanting to communicate and was absolutely not the message that was heard by the people watching from the temple. In Jewish history, there had been at least two major Jewish revolts against the authorities that every school boy would know all about: the Bar Kochba Revolt and the first Jewish War. What is important to know is that those revolts used the same symbol to represent the dream of Jewish independence. It was such a well-known symbol it was actually printed on the shekel, one of the common coins of the day. That symbol was the palm branch.

As the group grew and came to the top of the hill where they could easily be seen by the temple authorities and the Roman soldiers, they were yelling and waving the banner of independence, the symbol of revolution against the government and the temple. Adding to the confusion, some in the crowd began shouting and singing the words from Psalm 118, the words to be spoken as a new king entered the city, to drive out the enemies of the faith and to reclaim the temple and the land.

Was all of this part of Jesus' plan? Did he actually intend after three years of preaching and teaching that the kingdom of heaven was more important than any earthly kingdom, did he actually intend to end his ministry with a military parade?

This is where our passage of scripture begins this morning. In the middle of all that was happening on that hillside near Bethany, Philip, one of the disciples, was approached by a couple of Greeks who asked to speak with Jesus. These may have been Greek-speaking Jews who had come to town for the Passover, or they may have been non-Jewish Greeks who had heard about Jesus and wanted to speak with him. We just don't know. We do know that, as in the past, the disciples were still struggling. Philip didn't know what to do, so he went and found Andrew. Finally, at some point they told Jesus about the Greeks wanting to speak with him.

Suppose we could see Jesus' face as he responded. It would help to know if he smiled a bit when he heard about the Greeks, or if there was a hint of sadness in his eyes. Either everything was coming together as he had planned, and the stage was set for his grand finale, or he realized that things had gotten a bit out of control because people did not really understand him yet, and even his disciples were not ready for what was about to happen.

In my imagination, when he was told about the Greeks, Jesus took a deep breath and said, "The hour has come" (v. 23). I hear kind of a surrender, a recognition on his part that he had done everything he could do to prepare but it was now time for the big test. He said, "The time has come for the Son of Man to be glorified." His ministry had come to its end and the final step was to give up his life to help people understand. That was the only way they would grasp that he was not interested in being ruler of a temple or a country but was really talking about something beyond that. The fact that the Greeks had come to him showed that his message had taken seed and had begun to spread.

It probably got rather quiet as the guy everyone thought was leading the revolution lowered his head in prayer and asked his Father to save him from this hour. But, as in the Garden of Gethsemane, Jesus ended his prayer by saying, "But it is for this reason that I have come to this hour, so let it glorify your name" (vv. 27-28).

And as if God was making one final attempt to help the disciples understand, and to help everyone understand what Jesus was really all about, just then God spoke. John tells us that the crowd standing there actually heard it. The voice said: "I have glorified it, and I will glorify it again" (v. 28). It had to be an amazing moment when God actually spoke in order to help them understand.

And the result? Within a few minutes there was a huge argument taking place as people disagreed over what they had heard. Some said they heard God, others said it was just thunder. Jesus tried a few more times to explain what was going to happen but it was clear he understood that it was over. He had done what he could do. Just a few verses after our story today we're told that Jesus departed and hid from them all.

Jesus' public ministry ended on that hillside near Bethany. After all of his teaching, all his miracles, and all of his efforts to teach the disciples what was in his heart, it ended with him walking away and hiding. In what may be some of the saddest words in the gospel, John ended this story by saying: "Although he had performed so many signs in their presence, they did not believe in him" (v. 37).

I must say that there are many people who believe that Jesus was fully aware of what was going on and was not at all disappointed in what happened. Many people believe that he had actually planned everything to take place just as it did to fulfill a long list of prophesies from the Old Testament.

While this is possible, something else may be the case. It's possible that Jesus struggled with his ministry just as we constantly struggle with ours. Sometimes we just don't know if we've accomplished anything or not. Sometimes we are completely misunderstood and end up with things spiraling completely out of control, as people take something we say or do and use it for their own reasons. Sometimes we just want to walk away and hide from it all. That is the more preferable version of the story.

Because if it is true, and if God ended up taking what Jesus did and used it to change the world, then maybe there is still hope for what we're doing here today.

Passion / Palm Sunday
Mark 14:1—15:47

It was two days before the Passover and the festival of Unleavened Bread. The chief priests and the scribes were looking for a way to arrest Jesus by stealth and kill him; for they said, "Not during the festival, or there may be a riot among the people." While he was at Bethany in the house of Simon the leper, as he sat at the table, a woman came with an alabaster jar of very costly ointment of nard, and she broke open the jar and poured the ointment on his head. But some were there who said to one another in anger, "Why was the ointment wasted in this way? For this ointment could have been sold for more than three hundred denarii, and the money given to the poor." And they scolded her. But Jesus said, "Let her alone; why do you trouble her? She has performed a good service for me. For you always have the poor with you, and you can show kindness to them whenever you wish; but you will not always have me. She has done what she could; she has anointed my body beforehand for its burial. Truly I tell you, wherever the good news is proclaimed in the whole world, what she has done will be told in remembrance of her." Then Judas Iscariot, who was one of the twelve, went to the chief priests in order to betray him to them. When they heard it, they were greatly pleased, and promised to give him money. So he began to look for an opportunity to betray him. On the first day of Unleavened Bread, when the Passover lamb is sacrificed, his disciples said to him, "Where do you want us to go and make the preparations for you to eat the Passover?" So he sent two of his disciples, saying to them, "Go into the city, and a man carrying a jar of water will meet you; follow him, and wherever he enters, say to the owner of the house, 'The Teacher asks, Where is my guest room where I may eat the Passover with my disciples?' He will show you a large room upstairs, furnished and ready. Make preparations for us there." So the disciples set out and went to the city, and found everything as he had told them; and they prepared the Passover meal. When it was evening, he came with the twelve. And when they had taken their places and were eating, Jesus said, "Truly I tell you, one of you will betray me, one who is eating with me." They began to be distressed and to say to him one after another, "Surely, not I?" He said to them, "It is one of the twelve, one who is dipping bread into the bowl with me. For the Son of Man goes as it is written of him, but woe to that one by whom the Son of Man is betrayed! It would have been better for that one not to have been born." While they were eating, he took a loaf of bread, and after blessing it he broke it, gave it to them, and said, "Take; this is my body." Then he took a cup, and after giving thanks he gave it to them, and all of them drank from it. He said to them, "This is my blood of the covenant, which is poured out for many. Truly I tell you, I will never again drink of the fruit of the vine until that day when I drink it new in the kingdom of God." When they had sung the hymn, they went out to the Mount of Olives. And Jesus said to them, "You will all become deserters; for it is written, 'I will strike the shepherd, and the sheep will be scattered.' But after I am raised up, I will go before you to Galilee." Peter said to him, "Even though all become deserters, I will not." Jesus said to him, "Truly I tell you, this day, this very night, before the cock crows twice, you will deny me three times." But he said vehemently, "Even though I must die with you, I will not deny you." And all of them said the same. They went to a place called Gethsemane; and he said to his disciples, "Sit here while I pray." He took with him Peter and James and John, and began to be distressed and agitated. And he said to them, "I am deeply grieved, even to death; remain here, and keep awake." And going a little farther, he threw himself on the ground and prayed that, if it were possible, the hour might pass from him. He said, "Abba, Father, for you all things are possible; remove this cup from me; yet, not what I want, but what you want." He came and found them sleeping; and he said to Peter, "Simon, are you asleep? Could you not keep awake one hour? Keep awake and pray that you may not come into the time of trial; the spirit indeed is willing, but the flesh is weak." And again he went away and prayed, saying the same words. And once more he came and found them sleeping, for their eyes were very heavy; and they did not know what to say to him. He came a third time and said to them, "Are you still sleeping and taking your rest? Enough! The hour has come; the Son of Man is betrayed into the hands of sinners. Get up, let us be going. See, my betrayer is at hand." Immediately, while he was still speaking, Judas, one of the twelve, arrived; and with him there was a crowd with swords and clubs, from the chief priests, the scribes, and the elders. Now the betrayer had given them a sign, saying, "The one I will kiss is the man; arrest him and lead him away under guard." So when he came, he went up to him at once and said, "Rabbi!" and kissed him. Then they laid hands on him and arrested him. But one of those who stood near drew his sword and struck the slave of the high priest, cutting off his ear. Then Jesus said to them, "Have you come out with swords and clubs to arrest me as though I were a bandit? Day after day I was with you in the temple teaching, and you did not arrest me. But let the scriptures be fulfilled." All of them deserted him and fled. A certain young man was following him, wearing nothing but a linen cloth. They caught hold of him, but he left the linen cloth and ran off naked. They took Jesus to the high priest; and all the chief priests, the elders, and the scribes were assembled. Peter had followed him at a distance, right into the courtyard of the high priest; and he was sitting with the guards, warming himself at the fire. Now the chief priests and the whole council were looking for testimony against Jesus to put him to death; but they found none. For many gave false testimony against him, and their testimony did not agree. Some stood up and gave false testimony against him, saying, "We heard him say, 'I will destroy this temple that is made with hands, and in three days I will build another, not made with hands.' " But even on this point their testimony did not agree. Then the high priest stood up before them and asked Jesus, "Have you no answer? What is it that they testify against you?" But he was silent and did not answer. Again the high priest asked him, "Are you the Messiah, the Son of the Blessed One?" Jesus said, "I am; and 'you will see the Son of Man seated at the right hand of the Power,' and 'coming with the clouds of heaven.' " Then the high priest tore his clothes and said, "Why do we still need witnesses? You have heard his blasphemy! What is your decision?" All of them condemned him as deserving death. Some began to spit on him, to blindfold him, and to strike him, saying to him, "Prophesy!" The guards also took him over and beat him. While Peter was below in the courtyard, one of the servant-girls of the high priest came by. When she saw Peter warming himself, she stared at him and said, "You also were with Jesus, the man from Nazareth." But he denied it, saying, "I do not know or understand what you are talking about." And he went out into the forecourt. Then the cock crowed. And the servant-girl, on seeing him, began again to say to the bystanders, "This man is one of them." But again he denied it. Then after a little while the bystanders again said to Peter, "Certainly you are one of them; for you are a Galilean." But he began to curse, and he swore an oath, "I do not know this man you are talking about." At that moment the cock crowed for the second time. Then Peter remembered that Jesus had said to him, "Before the cock crows twice, you will deny me three times." And he broke down and wept.

As soon as it was morning, the chief priests held a consultation with the elders and scribes and the whole council. They bound Jesus, led him away, and handed him over to Pilate. Pilate asked him, "Are you the King of the Jews?" He answered him, "You say so." Then the chief priests accused him of many things. Pilate asked him again, "Have you no answer? See how many charges they bring against you." But Jesus made no further reply, so that Pilate was amazed. Now at the festival he used to release a prisoner for them, anyone for whom they asked. Now a man called Barabbas was in prison with the rebels who had committed murder during the insurrection. So the crowd came and began to ask Pilate to do for them according to his custom. Then he answered them, "Do you want me to release for you the King of the Jews?" For he realized that it was out of jealousy that the chief priests had handed him over. But the chief priests stirred up the crowd to have him release Barabbas for them instead. Pilate spoke to them again, "Then what do you wish me to do with the man you call the King of the Jews?" They shouted back, "Crucify him!" Pilate asked them, "Why, what evil has he done?" But they shouted all the more, "Crucify him!" So Pilate, wishing to satisfy the crowd, released Barabbas for them; and after flogging Jesus, he handed him over to be crucified. Then the soldiers led him into the courtyard of the palace (that is, the governor's headquarters); and they called together the whole cohort. And they clothed him in a purple cloak; and after twisting some thorns into a crown, they put it on him. And they began saluting him, "Hail, King of the Jews!" They struck his head with a reed, spat upon him, and knelt down in homage to him. After mocking him, they stripped him of the purple cloak and put his own clothes on him. Then they led him out to crucify him. They compelled a passer-by, who was coming in from the country, to carry his cross; it was Simon of Cyrene, the father of Alexander and Rufus. Then they brought Jesus to the place called Golgotha (which means the place of a skull). And they offered him wine mixed with myrrh; but he did not take it. And they crucified him, and divided his clothes among them, casting lots to decide what each should take. It was nine o'clock in the morning when they crucified him. The inscription of the charge against him read, "The King of the Jews." And with him they crucified two bandits, one on his right and one on his left. Those who passed by derided him, shaking their heads and saying, "Aha! You who would destroy the temple and build it in three days, save yourself, and come down from the cross!" In the same way the chief priests, along with the scribes, were also mocking him among themselves and saying, "He saved others; he cannot save himself. Let the Messiah, the King of Israel, come down from the cross now, so that we may see and believe." Those who were crucified with him also taunted him. When it was noon, darkness came over the whole land until three in the afternoon. At three o'clock Jesus cried out with a loud voice, "Eloi, Eloi, lema sabachthani?" which means, "My God, my God, why have you forsaken me?" When some of the bystanders heard it, they said, "Listen, he is calling for Elijah." And someone ran, filled a sponge with sour wine, put it on a stick, and gave it to him to drink, saying, "Wait, let us see whether Elijah will come to take him down." Then Jesus gave a loud cry and breathed his last. And the curtain of the temple was torn in two, from top to bottom. Now when the centurion, who stood facing him, saw that in this way he breathed his last, he said, "Truly this man was God's Son!" There were also women looking on from a distance; among them were Mary Magdalene, and Mary the mother of James the younger and of Joses, and Salome. These used to follow him and provided for him when he was in Galilee; and there were many other women who had come up with him to Jerusalem. When evening had come, and since it was the day of Preparation, that is, the day before the sabbath, Joseph of Arimathea, a respected

member of the council, who was also himself waiting ex-
pectantly for the kingdom of God, went boldly to Pilate and
asked for the body of Jesus. Then Pilate wondered if he were
already dead; and summoning the centurion, he asked him
whether he had been dead for some time. When he learned
from the centurion that he was dead, he granted the body to
Joseph. Then Joseph bought a linen cloth, and taking down
the body, wrapped it in the linen cloth, and laid it in a tomb
that had been hewn out of the rock. He then rolled a stone
against the door of the tomb. Mary Magdalene and Mary the
mother of Joses saw where the body was laid.

The Week

Note to the preacher:
This message is not presented as a sermon with an introduction, three points, and a conclusion, though you are welcome to rewrite it that way if you wish. My goal for this message is to invite my listeners to experience the events of Jesus' week, more as he and his disciples experienced them. This message takes us to the arrest in the orchard of Gethsemane. The messages for Maundy Thursday, Good Friday, and Easter Sunday will complete the journey. My goal was not to explain the stories or use them to create a series of conclusions or points, but to experience the stories once again, and allow God's voice to add any additional input that might be helpful. Imagine the following presented in the format of a movie with the screen quietly fading to black between each part of the story. A brief, silent pause will provide that for your listeners if you choose to follow my approach. However you choose to use the following story, I encourage you to leave room for the other great storyteller to join in.

(fade up)
The city is busy with thousands of people making final preparations for the Passover celebrations. The streets and marketplaces are crowded. As you walk around your eyes and ears are overwhelmed with everything going on as thousands of people from all over the world return to celebrate the holiday in Jerusalem. It is a serious time, but also a joyous partytime as families get together for huge feasts and activities for everyone from the oldest to the youngest. Kitchens are busy with amazing foods being prepared, living rooms are filled with people and stories as family members make up for the time they've been apart. Everywhere you look are the children, running and playing, filled with excitement and wonder as they wait for the mysterious events that are about to take place.

(fade out, pause, then up)
There is a small, dark room in a corner of the temple where it is quiet. A small group of men is speaking in hushed voices. Their quietness is not out of respect for the location in the temple but because they are talking about things they don't want anyone else to hear. They are the leaders of the faith, the priests of the temple, and the scribes responsible for protecting the Jewish law. They have a problem they need to fix.

(fade out, pause, then up)
At the top of the Mount of Olives, which is a hill just across the valley from the city, is the little village of Bethany. In Bethany there is another room filled with people who have gathered for the holiday, most of them traveling many miles from the north to be here. Jesus is reclining at the dinner table with the rest of the group, watching closely as Mary walks over to him, takes a small vial of very expensive perfume from the cord around her neck, and pours it over Jesus' head. In his version of the story, John tells us that it was Judas who spoke up first, but Mark says there were several in the group who became angry, upset that the expensive oil had been "wasted" and could instead have been sold and the money given to the poor. They had apparently missed the point that every Jewish woman carried the small vial around their necks. That vial was filled with as expensive perfume as she could afford. It wasn't for vanity, but it was to ensure that when she died they would have the proper oil and perfume available so she was certain to have a proper anointing when she was buried. Along with the others in the room, Judas was not impressed with the amazing sacrifice she made or the symbolism it carried.

(fade out, pause, then up)
The quietness of the priests and scribes in that small temple

hideout is broken when they hear someone approaching and opening the small door into the room. We don't know if they were actually surprised when they recognized Judas coming through the door. But it brought smiles to their faces as they realized they would now finally have the information they needed to solve their problem once and for all to protect their faith and their jobs. All it took was the promise of a little bit of money — a few coins. Just enough to make Judas feel a little better after seeing that waste of the oil poured over Jesus' head in that room in Bethany.

(fade out, pause, then up)
The disciples had spent a busy day running around making final preparations for the Passover celebration. They all finally gathered again in a room filled with cushions and a table set up in the middle of the room to recline around and enjoy the feast. If it was like the other gatherings taking place around town, they were telling stories, old and new, and following the familiar steps of the traditional Passover seder meal — traditional until the time that Jesus paused and said that one of them in the room was going to betray him. As the disciples registered shock and began to look at the others gathered in the room, many of whom they did not know, Jesus added that the one who would betray him was actually reclining at the table, eating the meal with him. Now they added their voices to their looking, each of them saying, "Surely, not I?" Jesus then added, "It is one of the twelve, one who is dipping bread into the bowl with me" (14:20). The Passover seder was a unique meal, and the food was set out so that each bowl was shared between two people. This narrowed down who Jesus was referring to as the one dipping into the bowl with him. Mark never actually told us who that person was, but just said it would actually be better for that person if they had never even been born. This is the point at which the other gospel writers tell us that Jesus then

looks at Judas sitting next to him and says, "What you are going to do, go and do quickly," and Judas gets up and runs from the room.

(fade out, pause, then up)

As the seder meal begins, the host takes a piece of bread and tears it into pieces. The pieces are then hidden. In more formal meals, the piece of bread was just hidden underneath the other pieces on the plate. But for family meals that included children, the pieces of bread were sometimes hidden in various places around the room. At the end of the meal, the children were sent to search for the hidden pieces, which were then brought back to the table and passed around as a dessert. We're not told how it was done this time, but we do know that when the lost pieces of bread were found, instead of just eating them as dessert, Mark tells us that Jesus passed the bread around and called it his body.

Throughout the meal, there had been a cup of wine that had been poured and left sitting on the table. As the meal came to a close, the doors to the house were opened up and several verses from the psalms were recited. According to tradition, this is the invitation for the prophet Elijah to come in and join the group. Elijah had lived during the rule of King Ahab in the ninth century BC. He performed many miracles, including raising someone from the dead, and at the end of his life we're told he was carried away into heaven by a whirlwind. That cup of wine on the table was called the Elijah cup. Since the prophecy said Elijah would return to the earth as a sign that the Messiah was about to arrive, the cup was put there for him to drink when he arrived. That cup was to be left untouched. But that night, Mark tells us that Jesus picked up the Elijah cup and drank from it. He then passed it around the table and told everyone that it was his blood. Mark does not tell us if the disciples really understood any of what Jesus was doing.

After the Passover meal, the group walked through the streets of the city, which would have been filled with other people out stretching their legs after the huge Passover meal. It would have been easy to pass unnoticed in the crowd, since everyone had enjoyed many cups of wine during the seder and were stuffed from the huge feast. At some point as they walked to the edge of the city near the Mount of Olives, Jesus said that they would all betray him. In fact, he said that before the sun came up in the morning, Peter would actually betray him three times. Peter insisted it was not true, and they all argued with him and insisted they would all remain true to him forever and follow him to the end of the world.

(fade out, pause, then up)
Gethsemane is a small olive orchard at the bottom of the Kidron Valley between Jerusalem and the Mount of Olives near where the town of Bethany sits. It was as safe a place as any for Jesus and the disciples to stop. Mark tells us that Jesus told the group to sit down while he prayed, and then took Peter, James, and John with him to another part of the garden. Jesus began to get upset, saying "I am deeply grieved, even to death" and asked the three of them to stay there while he prayed. Jesus walked a little further by himself and prayed. Mark tells us he began his prayer with the word *Abba*, which most people translate as meaning "Father." But that is not quite accurate. The word *Abba* is the same word used by little children even today when they talk with their father. The more accurate translation would actually be "Daddy." So Mark tells us that Jesus threw himself on the ground and prayed, "Daddy, anything is possible for you. So, please take all of this away from me." He paused, and we can imagine he took a slow, deep breath, and then said, "But, it's not important what I want, but what you want."

Jesus got up from the ground and went back to the three disciples, who were sound asleep. Jesus asked them to stay awake and pray about the trial that was about to come, then he went to pray. When he came back they were asleep. This happened a third time. We have to be fair to the disciples here. First, they really didn't understand what was going on, nor what this trial was that Jesus was talking about. Second, they had just finished a huge meal with several glasses of wine. So these guys would have had a really tough time staying awake even if they did understand what was about to happen.

(fade out, pause, then up)
As Jesus was talking with the three disciples, they saw Judas quickly enter the Gethsemane orchard. With him was a group of people carrying swords, clubs, and torches. Some versions of the story suggest that these were some of the priests and scribes who had come to arrest Jesus, but Mark is clear that these folks were *from* the priests and scribes. Judas had brought a group of thugs to get Jesus. These were people who knew how to do the job and would do whatever they needed to do to earn their pay. Judas walked over to Jesus, called him *teacher*, and kissed him, which was the prearranged sign to the mob. A brief scuffle ensued, and one of the disciples pulled a sword and cut off the ear of one of the guys in the crowd; we're told it was one of the slaves of the high priest. Before things got completely out of hand, Jesus spoke up and distracted them with a little sarcasm. The members of the mob refocused their energy on doing what they had come to do.

It all happened very quickly, so it may have been easy to miss a couple of interesting things that took place. First, one of the disciples was carrying a sword. We knew that Judas was a Zealot, and like all Zealots, carried a small knife to poke into any Roman soldier if the opportunity presented itself. But Judas was on the other team this time. Tradition suggests it was Simon Peter who carried the sword. We honestly don't know, but as we think about everything else we've seen and heard from Peter, being that hothead who acts and speaks before he thinks, it does make sense that it could have been him. In one way, it was kind of a nice reinforcement of Peter's insistence an hour or so ago that he would never betray Jesus and would stay with him forever. Yet as soon as Jesus stopped the scuffle, what happened next? After all of that talk an hour or so ago about never betraying him, Mark simply tells us "all of them deserted him and fled" (Mark 14:50).

(fade out, pause, then up)
Palm Sunday is a day we traditionally celebrate what we refer to as the "triumphal entry" of Jesus into Jerusalem. We wave palm branches and sing songs of peace and joy, thinking about all that Jesus has said and done during his three years of active ministry leading up to this day. We talk about the priests and the scribes and their dirty deeds, and how satisfying it is to see the image of Jesus walking into their temple and throwing things around in his righteous anger. We can close our eyes and fantasize about doing that same thing in many of our own situations today. Palm Sunday is traditionally a day we celebrate a coming victory, and see it as the final announcement that Jesus is about to change the world.

While there was celebration on Sunday, that celebration may not have been what Jesus had in mind at all. He had come to change the world, there's no question about that. But it's possible no one really understood just what that meant, so how could they celebrate it?

Let's move from Palm Sunday to Easter morning one step at a time. Today, let's keep our thoughts on the amazing transition from the day people gathered on the hillside

waving palm branches and singing psalms of praise, to the late night just a few days later that everyone was gone, and the ones closest to him who had promised to remain with him to the ends of the earth had just run off into the darkness to save their own hides. This is real. This is the week that Jesus lived. This is a part of our experience as a people of faith.
(fade)

Maundy Thursday
John 13:1-17, 31b-35

Now before the festival of the Passover, Jesus knew that his hour had come to depart from this world and go to the Father. Having loved his own who were in the world, he loved them to the end. The devil had already put it into the heart of Judas son of Simon Iscariot to betray him. And during supper Jesus, knowing that the Father had given all things into his hands, and that he had come from God and was going to God, got up from the table, took off his outer robe, and tied a towel around himself. Then he poured water into a basin and began to wash the disciples' feet and to wipe them with the towel that was tied around him. He came to Simon Peter, who said to him, "Lord, are you going to wash my feet?" Jesus answered, "You do not know now what I am doing, but later you will understand." Peter said to him, "You will never wash my feet." Jesus answered, "Unless I wash you, you have no share with me." Simon Peter said to him, "Lord, not my feet only but also my hands and my head!" Jesus said to him, "One who has bathed does not need to wash, except for the feet, but is entirely clean. And you are clean, though not all of you." For he knew who was to betray him; for this reason he said, "Not all of you are clean." After he had washed their feet, had put on his robe, and had returned to the table, he said to them, "Do you know what I have done to you? You call me Teacher and Lord — and you are right, for that is what I am. So if I, your Lord and Teacher, have washed your feet, you also ought to wash one another's feet. For I have set you an example, that you also should do as I have done to you. Very truly, I tell you, servants are not greater than their master, nor are messengers greater than the one who sent them. If you know these things, you are blessed if you do them.... When he had gone out, Jesus said, "Now the Son of Man has been glorified, and God has been glorified in him. If God has been glorified in him, God will also glorify him in himself and will glorify him at once. Little children, I am with you only a little longer. You will look for me; and as I said to the Jews so now I say to you, 'Where I am going, you cannot come.' I give you a new commandment, that you love one another. Just as I have loved you, you also should love one another. By this everyone will know that you are my disciples, if you have love for one another."

Where It Ends

All of the plans and preparation had been completed and they were all gathering together in the room. As they entered, they each paused to look at the long, horseshoe-shaped table with the cushions spread out around the outside, and could not help but show a brief smile. Even with everything that had happened and with the risks they faced out in the streets, the sight of that table and cushions took all of that away for a few seconds.

Before they were disciples, they had all been part of good Jewish families and had all grown up with years of memories around the Passover seder meal. The meal was built entirely around a very serious ritual, designed to ensure that the stories of Moses and the Exodus from Egypt were remembered from generation to generation. As serious as the intent, the evening itself was filled with good fun and family fellowship and was an exciting time for everyone of every age. Some of their earliest memories were of being sent out after the meal to search for the hidden pieces of matzo that would be a part of the dessert. The fact that the pieces also reminded them of how God found the people in their bondage and rescued them is something they understood later.

As they looked around the room, they remembered their many experiences around the seder table. And as they moved to find their seats, they all knew exactly what was coming, just as they had experienced the seder so many times before.

Everyone gathered around the low table and took their positions, stretched out on the cushions, reclining on their left sides with their heads near the table and their legs stretched out toward the walls behind them. It was the position of royalty, and something the slaves in Egypt did during that very first Passover seder long ago to symbolize their coming change in status.

The head of the family, or host, would recline in the center position, say the ritual prayers, and perform the same actions that were performed every year. After a brief welcome and greeting, servants would come into the room carrying bowls of water and towels, and would slowly move along the wall behind the table, pausing to carefully wash the feet of each guest and then gently dry them with their towel. It was partly symbolic, and partly just a good idea. The act was a symbolic message from the host that each guest was welcomed into the place and that everything would be done to make them feel comfortable as an honored guest. Additionally, since everyone had spent their day walking the dusty roads and streets of Jerusalem, a good foot washing was an act promoting good hygiene.

After the ritual of washing the feet, the host of the meal would begin the ceremony itself. There were several prayers, stories, and recitations by everyone at the table. It included the eating of specific foods, herbs, and spices, each recalling a taste or smell that rekindled memories of the Passover story, along with several glasses of wine, also representing important elements of the story. As they found their comfortable spot on the cushions, we can hear them all chatting in anticipation of the familiar experience they were undertaking together.

Then it got very quiet.

Jesus had spoken the familiar words to welcome everyone and the first glass of wine had been shared. At first, no one paid any attention to Jesus getting up from his place at the table and leaving the room. It was not unusual at all, because even as important as the seder is, the overall atmosphere is pretty casual. While he was out, the chatter had begun again as they recalled stories from past seders together. The quietness came in stages, only as each person in the room noticed what was happening. If you picture it, with everyone leaning on their left side, some of the group were most likely facing away from the door and did not see Jesus when he first returned to the room. They were still chatting away, having a grand time, until others at the table hushed them and pointed toward the door. Then the silence was complete — silence and some very real confusion.

Jesus was walking back into the room, carrying a large bowl of water. His outer robe was gone, and he had a towel tied around his waist. He almost looked like one of the servants. The rest of the servants were standing behind him, shifting from one foot to the other in the same cloud of confusion as the disciples around the table. What was happening here? This was not how the ritual went. Instead of the servants coming in to wash everyone's feet, it actually appeared that — no — of course not — it was just too nonsensical to even consider.

Jesus walked along behind the table and stopped at the outstretched legs of a disciple. He bent down on his knees and carefully cupped water from the bowl with his hands. He poured it over the feet of the startled disciple. He slowly wiped the water away with the towel, and then reached for the small vial of perfume oil. He poured a small amount of oil into his hands and then massaged it into the tired and sore feet of the disciple. When he was finished, he calmly repositioned himself behind the next disciple, and then the next, and continued in the same manner around the table.

No words were being spoken and there were glances as the disciples looked at each other around the table, trying to make sense of what was happening. It made absolutely no sense. The foot washing was a job for the servants, those people who weren't sitting at the table, and whose primary reason for being there was to serve everyone else. To think that anyone with the privilege of having a place at the table would even think of giving it up to act like a servant was unheard of. And to think that the host himself was doing that! No — it made no sense at all. But no one even knew how to ask about it or protest. One disciple did pull his legs back, perhaps out of embarrassment at what Jesus was doing, but Jesus simply smiled and calmly reached out and pulled the guy's feet toward him so he could complete his task.

Then Jesus came to Peter at the end of the table. If Peter had a thought on his mind he spoke it, even if that thought was better left unspoken. In this case, as Jesus moved to pour his handful of water onto Peter's feet, Peter did not just pull his legs away, but he sat up from the table and asked, "Lord, are you going to wash my feet?" (v. 6). Jesus calmly replied that he realized Peter did not understand what was happening but assured him that he would understand everything later. In the quietness of that moment, Peter almost shouted at Jesus: "You will never wash *my* feet!" (v. 8).

All eyes were on Jesus, to see how he would respond.

Rather than argue, or try to complete the act against Peter's will, Jesus calmly looked him in the eye and said, "Unless I wash you, you have no share with me" (v. 8).

It suddenly grew very cold in the room. It was one of those key moments in which a decision had to be made that had some very big consequences. Peter still could not imagine what Jesus was doing and the true meaning of it did not even cross his mind. All that Peter understood was that he had a choice either to stay with Jesus or be left behind. Peter responded in the only way he knew how.

Peter said, "Lord, not my feet only but also my hands and my head!" (v. 9). That's Peter for you. It's all or nothing, no middle ground on anything. Undoubtedly, that comment broke the tension in the room, and I can see all of the other disciples almost bursting out in laughter, "Yep, that's Peter for you!" I even see a smile on Jesus' face. Even though Peter is completely lost here and has absolutely no idea of what is actually going on, Jesus admired the raw honesty that Peter has and had a smile on his face as he said, "One who has bathed does not need to wash, except for the feet." I can see Peter very slowly unfolding his legs and stretching his feet out where Jesus can reach them. I can see the almost painful look on Peter's face as Jesus poured the water and wiped with the towel. I can see Peter almost visibly shaking as Jesus massaged that perfume oil on his feet. In my imagination, as he finished, Jesus gave Peter's feet a little pat, just to say, "There, that wasn't so bad, was it?"

After leaving to change again, and then returning to the room and his place as the host of the seder meal, Jesus asked if they knew just what it was that he had just done. Apparently, no one did, or at least couldn't imagine saying it out loud. So Jesus explained. "You call me Teacher and Lord, and you are right, because that is what I am. So if I, your Lord and Teacher, have washed your feet, you also ought to wash one another's feet. I have set for you an example that you also should do as I have done to you" (vv. 13-15).

The disciples glanced at one another, trying to imagine actually having to take the step of physically washing each other's feet. It was a rather difficult thing for them to imagine doing. Jesus apparently saw their hesitation and tried to help clear away the symbolism of what he had done by simply explaining that even though he is their Lord and Teacher, he is still a servant of God. And a part of the role of God's servant is to serve others too, even if that sometimes means giving up your seat as host at the table and taking on the role of the lowest person in the room. Then he said, "If you know these things, you are blessed if you do them" (v. 17).

And that's where all of the trouble begins, isn't it?

Sometimes we're pretty hard on Peter and some of the other disciples. We remember stories like these that point out the sometimes-foolish and self-serving things that Peter said and did, and we remember how he eventually will run away and deny even knowing who Jesus was. In fact, they all end up running away. After all of their time with Jesus himself, they end up not being able to take the heat, and they run away.

When I start feeling too strongly about their actions, it helps me to be honest with myself. There are a lot of feet out there that I would simply refuse to wash myself. As Jesus said, I know these are things I should do, but I just won't do them. There are some people out there who's feet I am just not willing to wash.

Let's be clear. We're not talking about taking a bowl of water, a towel, and some perfume and being brave enough to touch someone's feet with it. As difficult as that act is for some of us, it's nowhere near what Jesus was actually talking about. While washing someone's feet can be a humbling, and a very serving act, it's not that kind of physical servant act that Jesus was describing that night in the room filled with cushions. He was talking about something more than physical. He was talking about an internal thing, and internal feeling, a feeling of personal value. What Jesus was challenging his disciples to understand was that the ones who will "have a share with him" are the ones who will treat all other people as having more value than they have themselves. It means that the disciples will set aside their position, and care for those with the lowest, or even no position. Jesus took the role of the lowest in the room and challenges us to do the exact same thing.

When I am being honest with myself, I have to admit that I'm no better at this than Peter or any of the other disciples were. There are people I just do not want to serve. I simply can't bring myself to do it. Most of us spend a significant amount of our time and energy attempting to improve our position, and the idea of doing the opposite makes as little sense to us as it did to Peter. Much of our day is defined by our position. Who we associate with, who we agree with, and who we want nothing to do with is greatly defined by our position and theirs. Is Jesus actually expecting us to take off the external robe we have spent so much time crafting and actually pick up the pieces of the position of those who are so far and different from us, who may believe things that we do not, and see ourselves as their servant? Seriously?

"If you know these things, you are blessed if you do them" (v. 17).

Try this. Create the picture in your mind of someone who is a problem for you, someone you don't like, or don't agree with. Think of someone whose life and life choices are so different from yours it just drives you crazy.

If someone asked you to wash that person's feet, it might be a difficult thing to do, but maybe if you closed your eyes, and tried really hard, you could get it done. You might not look them in the eyes before, during, or afterward and might never admit later that you did it, but you could do it.

But what if you were asked to take that same person and to honestly consider them as someone worth serving? What if you were asked to look at that person as someone with all the same rights and opportunities as you or anyone else? What if you were asked to accept the fact that they have exactly the same value as you? What if you were asked to care about them? And *for* them?

Sometimes, that's where it all comes to an end, isn't it?

Peter was a strong man and strong in his beliefs. He sat through the rest of that seder meal trying to imagine just how in the world he could ever bring himself to serve a Gentile, let alone a Roman. I doubt he tasted a thing. Like Peter, I am beginning to understand just how difficult it is to actually have a share of what Jesus offered.

Good Friday
John 18:1—19:42

After Jesus had spoken these words, he went out with his disciples across the Kidron Valley to a place where there was a garden, which he and his disciples entered. Now Judas, who betrayed him, also knew the place, because Jesus often met there with his disciples. So Judas brought a detachment of soldiers together with police from the chief priests and the Pharisees, and they came there with lanterns and torches and weapons. Then Jesus, knowing all that was to happen to him, came forward and asked them, "Whom are you looking for?" They answered, "Jesus of Nazareth." Jesus replied, "I am he." Judas, who betrayed him, was standing with them. When Jesus said to them, "I am he," they stepped back and fell to the ground. Again he asked them, "Whom are you looking for?" And they said, "Jesus of Nazareth." Jesus answered, "I told you that I am he. So if you are looking for me, let these men go." This was to fulfill the word that he had spoken, "I did not lose a single one of those whom you gave me." Then Simon Peter, who had a sword, drew it, struck the high priest's slave, and cut off his right ear. The slave's name was Malchus. Jesus said to Peter, "Put your sword back into its sheath. Am I not to drink the cup that the Father has given me?" So the soldiers, their officer, and the Jewish police arrested Jesus and bound him. First they took him to Annas, who was the father-in-law of Caiaphas, the high priest that year. Caiaphas was the one who had advised the Jews that it was better to have one person die for the people. Simon Peter and another disciple followed Jesus. Since that disciple was known to the high priest, he went with Jesus into the courtyard of the high priest, but Peter was standing outside at the gate. So the other disciple, who was known to the high priest, went out, spoke to the woman who guarded the gate, and brought Peter in. The woman said to Peter,

"You are not also one of this man's disciples, are you?" He said, "I am not." Now the slaves and the police had made a charcoal fire because it was cold, and they were standing around it and warming themselves. Peter also was standing with them and warming himself. Then the high priest questioned Jesus about his disciples and about his teaching. Jesus answered, "I have spoken openly to the world; I have always taught in synagogues and in the temple, where all the Jews come together. I have said nothing in secret. Why do you ask me? Ask those who heard what I said to them; they know what I said." When he had said this, one of the police standing nearby struck Jesus on the face, saying, "Is that how you answer the high priest?" Jesus answered, "If I have spoken wrongly, testify to the wrong. But if I have spoken rightly, why do you strike me?" Then Annas sent him bound to Caiaphas the high priest. Now Simon Peter was standing and warming himself. They asked him, "You are not also one of his disciples, are you?" He denied it and said, "I am not." One of the slaves of the high priest, a relative of the man whose ear Peter had cut off, asked, "Did I not see you in the garden with him?" Again Peter denied it, and at that moment the cock crowed. Then they took Jesus from Caiaphas to Pilate's headquarters. It was early in the morning. They themselves did not enter the headquarters, so as to avoid ritual defilement and to be able to eat the Passover. So Pilate went out to them and said, "What accusation do you bring against this man?" They answered, "If this man were not a criminal, we would not have handed him over to you." Pilate said to them, "Take him yourselves and judge him according to your law." The Jews replied, "We are not permitted to put anyone to death." (This was to fulfill what Jesus had said when he indicated the kind of death he was to die.) Then Pilate entered the headquarters again, summoned Jesus, and asked him, "Are you the King of the Jews?" Jesus answered, "Do you ask this on your own, or did others tell

you about me?" Pilate replied, "I am not a Jew, am I? Your own nation and the chief priests have handed you over to me. What have you done?" Jesus answered, "My kingdom is not from this world. If my kingdom were from this world, my followers would be fighting to keep me from being handed over to the Jews. But as it is, my kingdom is not from here." Pilate asked him, "So you are a king?" Jesus answered, "You say that I am a king. For this I was born, and for this I came into the world, to testify to the truth. Everyone who belongs to the truth listens to my voice." Pilate asked him, "What is truth?" After he had said this, he went out to the Jews again and told them, "I find no case against him. But you have a custom that I release someone for you at the Passover. Do you want me to release for you the King of the Jews?" They shouted in reply, "Not this man, but Barabbas!" Now Barabbas was a bandit.

Then Pilate took Jesus and had him flogged. And the soldiers wove a crown of thorns and put it on his head, and they dressed him in a purple robe. They kept coming up to him, saying, "Hail, King of the Jews!" and striking him on the face. Pilate went out again and said to them, "Look, I am bringing him out to you to let you know that I find no case against him." So Jesus came out, wearing the crown of thorns and the purple robe. Pilate said to them, "Here is the man!" When the chief priests and the police saw him, they shouted, "Crucify him! Crucify him!" Pilate said to them, "Take him yourselves and crucify him; I find no case against him." The Jews answered him, "We have a law, and according to that law he ought to die because he has claimed to be the Son of God." Now when Pilate heard this, he was more afraid than ever. He entered his headquarters again and asked Jesus, "Where are you from?" But Jesus gave him no answer. Pilate therefore said to him, "Do you refuse to speak to me? Do you not know that I have power to release you, and power to crucify you?" Jesus answered him, "You would *have no power over me unless it had been given you from above; therefore the one who handed me over to you is guilty of a greater sin." From then on Pilate tried to release him, but the Jews cried out, "If you release this man, you are no friend of the emperor. Everyone who claims to be a king sets himself against the emperor." When Pilate heard these words, he brought Jesus outside and sat on the judge's bench at a place called The Stone Pavement, or in Hebrew Gabbatha. Now it was the day of Preparation for the Passover; and it was about noon. He said to the Jews, "Here is your King!" They cried out, "Away with him! Away with him! Crucify him!" Pilate asked them, "Shall I crucify your King?" The chief priests answered, "We have no king but the emperor." Then he handed him over to them to be crucified. So they took Jesus; and carrying the cross by himself, he went out to what is called The Place of the Skull, which in Hebrew is called Golgotha. There they crucified him, and with him two others, one on either side, with Jesus between them. Pilate also had an inscription written and put on the cross. It read, "Jesus of Nazareth, the King of the Jews." Many of the Jews read this inscription, because the place where Jesus was crucified was near the city; and it was written in Hebrew, in Latin, and in Greek. Then the chief priests of the Jews said to Pilate, "Do not write, 'The King of the Jews,' but, 'This man said, I am King of the Jews.'" Pilate answered, "What I have written I have written." When the soldiers had crucified Jesus, they took his clothes and divided them into four parts, one for each soldier. They also took his tunic; now the tunic was seamless, woven in one piece from the top. So they said to one another, "Let us not tear it, but cast lots for it to see who will get it." This was to fulfill what the scripture says, "They divided my clothes among themselves, and for my clothing they cast lots." And that is what the soldiers did. Meanwhile, standing near the cross of Jesus were his mother, and his mother's sister, Mary the wife of Clopas, and Mary Magdalene. When*

Jesus saw his mother and the disciple whom he loved stand-
ing beside her, he said to his mother, "Woman, here is your
son." Then he said to the disciple, "Here is your mother."
And from that hour the disciple took her into his own home.
After this, when Jesus knew that all was now finished, he said
(in order to fulfill the scripture), "I am thirsty." A jar full of
sour wine was standing there. So they put a sponge full of the
wine on a branch of hyssop and held it to his mouth. When
Jesus had received the wine, he said, "It is finished." Then
he bowed his head and gave up his spirit. Since it was the
day of Preparation, the Jews did not want the bodies left on
the cross during the sabbath, especially because that sabbath
was a day of great solemnity. So they asked Pilate to have
the legs of the crucified men broken and the bodies removed.
Then the soldiers came and broke the legs of the first and of
the other who had been crucified with him. But when they
came to Jesus and saw that he was already dead, they did
not break his legs. Instead, one of the soldiers pierced his
side with a spear, and at once blood and water came out.
(He who saw this has testified so that you also may believe.
His testimony is true, and he knows that he tells the truth.)
These things occurred so that the scripture might be fulfilled,
"None of his bones shall be broken." And again another pas-
sage of scripture says, "They will look on the one whom they
have pierced." After these things, Joseph of Arimathea, who
was a disciple of Jesus, though a secret one because of his
fear of the Jews, asked Pilate to let him take away the body of
Jesus. Pilate gave him permission; so he came and removed
his body. Nicodemus, who had at first come to Jesus by night,
also came, bringing a mixture of myrrh and aloes, weighing
about a hundred pounds. They took the body of Jesus and
wrapped it with the spices in linen cloths, according to the
burial custom of the Jews. Now there was a garden in the
place where he was crucified, and in the garden there was

a new tomb in which no one had ever been laid. And so, because it was the Jewish day of Preparation, and the tomb was nearby, they laid Jesus there.

Out of Control

Note to the preacher:
As I write this message, my vision is that it is something more than just another sermon. It is written in four sections, each one presenting a step in the story of the events of that Friday. My personal presentation of this message would be in one of two ways, depending on the experience I am wanting to create. Option 1 would be to use this as the format for the entire Good Friday service, with each section of the story separated with music, liturgy, or any other activity desired. Option 2, which is my preference, is that the entire service is simply the message. The service begins in a lighted sanctuary with candles as desired. After each section of the story, a brief period of quiet and personal prayer is taken, while one section of lights and candles is quietly extinguished. As the final section of the story is completed, the last of the lights are extinguished, leaving the entire sanctuary in darkness, with the exception of one remaining "Candle of Hope" on the altar table. Everyone leaves the sanctuary in silence. There is no music, no scripted liturgy or common prayers, just the story. The experience is a simple recreation of the increasing darkness that was the day.

ONE

The main streets were crowded with people taking a long walk after the big seder celebration. Since this was the time when family members came back home from the far corners of the world, it would have been quite a sight, filled with colorful clothing and with a constant hum from the many conversations. But the disciples were not a part of that crowd. Judas had left during the meal, and no one was quite sure just what was going to happen next, so the group took the dark side streets and avoided the crowds as they made their way out of Jerusalem that night. It's likely that even though it was the biggest night of celebration of the year, the group was quiet as they walked.

Just as they had found the room where they had celebrated the seder meal, someone had made arrangements to get them the key to the gate of the small olive orchard near the bottom of the Kidron Valley, and as they went inside they each searched around for a comfortable place out of the breeze where they could get a good night's sleep. Jesus asked a couple of them to stay with him for a while, and they walked further into the orchard as Jesus tried to help them understand what was going to happen. It may have been the late hour, or maybe it was all the wine from the seder meal, but they had a hard time understanding what he was saying to them. After a few more minutes, Jesus asked them to sit down and pray while he spent a few minutes by himself. Once by himself, Jesus prayed about what was going to happen. He asked if there was any way it could all just be avoided and they could all go home again, but he ended by simply saying that he would do whatever he was asked to do. When he returned to the others, they were asleep.

As he was waking them up, before we really find out whether he was upset with them or understood their weariness, it was then that the locked gate to the orchard was opened and Judas walked through it. Behind him was a collection of others. Each gospel writer describes the group a bit differently, saying it was soldiers and police officers, or servants from the high priests and scribes, or a bunch of paid hoodlums sent to do the dirty work. Regardless, Judas pointed to Jesus, words were exchanged, Matthew says there was a brief scuffle that Jesus quickly ended, all leading to Jesus being taken from the olive orchard at Gethsemane, while the disciples stood still, wiping the sleep from their eyes.

TWO

John tells us that they walked back through the streets of town, actually traveling a good way across the city, ending up at the home of the Annas, the father-in-law of the current high priest of the temple. Why take him to Annas? Annas was in line to become the next high priest and had a vested interest in seeing that this situation be resolved as quickly and efficiently as possible. Was it the normal, legal step to take? Probably not, but this was one of those situations in which following the normal and legal process was seen as less important than getting it resolved.

According to tradition, Annas was either busy at a party of his own or was actually already in bed and had to be awakened. Either way, the tradition says that Jesus was temporarily put into a cell with other prisoners while they waited for Annas to get ready for him. Today, if you visit the site of Annas' house, you can still walk down the stone steps into the hole in the ground that served as the cell. The hole is about twenty feet square and approximately thirty feet deep. At the time it was used as a cell there were no stairs to walk down. When a prisoner was put into the cell, a trapdoor was opened at the top and he was simply dropped into the hole. When it was time for him to be tried, a rope was lowered into the hole for the prisoner to tie around his waist, and he was quickly pulled up. This was not a nice place. It had a mud floor and no conveniences. When a prisoner was yanked back up out of the pit, he was usually dowsed with just enough water to make him presentable, and then dealt with. After some unknown length of time, they hoisted Jesus up, took the rope off, and splashed him with a bucket of water before taking him to the now-prepared, high priest-to-be, Annas.

While this was happening, if we pull our view back a bit from the room, in that dark little space near the gate to Annas' house, we can see someone standing. It is Peter. The same Peter who had followed Jesus that first day along the shore of the Sea of Galilee had followed him this one more time. Just as we see him, someone else also noticed him, and recognized him as one of Jesus' followers. Peter quickly denied it, knowing that with things as they were he would be the next one thrown into that big hole in the floor. As they waited, it grew colder outside and Peter moved a little closer to the small fire that was burning near the gate. Again someone recognized him and again he pretended ignorance. The third time someone approached him, either from panic or just from exhaustion, Peter turned away.

Inside the house, Annas was faced with a serious problem. As great a threat as Jesus was, Annas had no authority to condemn him to death. Only the Roman authorities had that power, and Annas knew that Rome really wasn't interested in the theological concerns of the temple. All the Roman leaders wanted was to avoid any real political problems or any real threats that might get the attention of their leaders back in Rome. As long as they kept the political front quiet, they kept their jobs. After a brief conversation with Jesus, which most of the writers tell us was more a monologue than an actual conversation, Annas told the group to take Jesus to Caiaphas, the current high priest and let him figure it out.

John doesn't tell us much about the time with Caiaphas, but he was apparently smart enough to realize the real problem, so he quickly had Jesus dragged through the streets once again, this time to see Pilate, the local Roman official.

Pilate had little interest in, or patience for, all of this "Jewish religious stuff," and it was, after all, now the wee hours of the morning and since they had no real legal charges against this Jesus, he simply said, "Deal with him yourself!" The crowd grew restless and that got Pilate's attention. It looked like one of those situations that might erupt into a riot. It was a situation that might end up being heard about in Rome and costing him his job, so he realized he needed to resolve it then and there.

Whatever else Pilate was, he was no dummy. He had heard the crowd saying something about Jesus being the King of the Jews, and if someone was actually claiming to be a king, that could be considered the kind of political threat that would give him the ability to respond legally. As John tells the story, Pilate was walking over to where Jesus was being held, probably squinting his eyes as he saw the condition that Jesus was in after all that had already happened. Pilate spoke fairly calmly, almost friend-to-friend, saying, "So tell me, these folks say you are a king. Are you really the King of the Jews?" Can you see the little glint of light in Pilate's eyes as he waited for the answer? As soon as Jesus would admit it, Pilate could get this whole thing resolved, make the crowd happy, and get back to bed where he would rather be right now.

But try as he might, no matter how carefully Pilate phrased the question, Jesus just didn't play the game. He didn't admit it but neither did he deny it. Consequently, without a clear confession, Pilate had nothing on which to base a judgment. He was caught between trying to do the correct, legal thing and trying to satisfy the mob. You almost feel sorry for Pilate at this point — almost.

Pilate had one more idea that he thought might make this mess go away, so he reminded the crowd of the custom of freeing a prisoner on Passover. Why didn't they just free Jesus and be done with it all? But that backfired too, most likely because everyone there knew the tradition better than Pilate and had already made the plan to ask for Barabbas instead.

Finally, hoping that it might satisfy the crowd enough, Pilate ordered the soldiers to take Jesus to their fortress near the temple and flog him.

THREE

Things were quickly spiraling out of control. Regardless of any concern about legality that Pilate may have had, the average Roman soldier enjoyed any opportunity to punish a Jew. Jesus was taken to the open stone floor of the Antonia fortress for some savage entertainment in what was called "the King's Game." He was tied to a post, with his arms stretched around the pole in front of him. Soldiers rolled dice made of the bones of former prisoners and moved the game piece around the circle carved in the stone floor. The circle had pie-shape areas carved into it, each one with a drawing. Whichever drawing the soldier's token landed on determined what the soldier would do to the prisoner. If they landed on the image of the scourge, the soldier grabbed the little wooden stick with the long leather straps, each strap with a small piece of bone or metal tied to it, and they would whip the prisoner with it. If their token landed on the drawing of the robe, that soldier placed the old worn blanket on the prisoner's now bloody shoulders. And just for fun, they would then quickly pull it off again, reopening the fresh wounds from the scourging. If their token landed on the drawing of the crown, they took the pieces of hedge thorn that had been bent into a circle, and crammed it onto the prisoner's head. And if their token landed on the cross? Well, the rules were clear that you could not actually use the cross until all of the other things were done first. It was no fun if the game ended too soon.

Part way through the game, Pilate came to the fortress to see if the crowd was satisfied with the beating, and whether they would now go home and end the hassle. They were not ready for that. After more time and conversation, Pilate used the one remaining legal option he had available and told the servants to bring him a bowl of water and a towel. It was a simple ritual, and it may not have been legal. But as he washed his hands in the water, the message was that he was officially washing his hands of the entire matter and whatever the crowd wanted to do from here on was up to them. It was time for the one, last game piece to be played.

FOUR

Jesus was untied from the pole, and a large heavy piece of wood was loaded across his shoulders with his arms tied to it so it would not fall off. This would be fastened to another tall pole nearby and the two of them together would form the final cross from the King's Game. One more time Jesus was led through the streets of town, just now coming to life as morning stirred. These were the people who five days ago had stood along the roads waving palm branches.

The walk ended at the top of a small outcropping of rock, in the middle of a cemetery for wealthy Jews just outside the city walls. Since crucifixions were seen as an unclean act, it gave the Romans a special pleasure in performing them here, making this important Jewish site unclean in the process. It was one of those added bonuses for them.

According to rules and tradition, Jesus was then stripped of all clothing and made to lie down next to the pole that had been pulled out of its hole. His wooden cross piece was tied to the pole and then the two pieces of wood were slowly raised into the air, lifting Jesus up. For added strength, spikes had been driven through Jesus wrists and into the cross piece. Experience had taught the Romans that it was important to use the wrists, because the hands were too fragile and the victim might fall from the cross too early. The cross was slowly raised into its hole until gravity finally took over, and...

THUD!

The cross settled into place with a shock that tore at Jesus' wrists. Once the cross was vertical, the soldiers nailed another board below his waist and twisted his legs sideways to push his feet up under his buttocks, so they could nail them to that new board. This took some of the pressure off of Jesus' wrists, making it possible for him to remain on the cross for days, rather than hours. The twisted position he was now in also meant that while he could inhale and take in a good breath, he now had to pull with his wrists to straighten himself enough to exhale. Most victims of crucifixion actually died very slowly of asphyxiation, finally becoming too exhausted to exhale. However wonderfully it is represented by the great artistic masters throughout history, crucifixion has nothing beautiful about it whatsoever.

The soldiers ended their King's Game the same way as always, gathering around under the cross to throw the dice again, to determine which of them got to keep anything of value the victim would no longer need.

At some point, Jesus asked for a drink, and a soldier stepped forward with a sponge on a stick, soaked with wine. Since the alcohol actually served as a mild pain-killer, this almost seems to be a rare act of kindness in the middle of all of the horror. However, by easing the pain, the victim might actually remain hanging up there even longer for everyone to see and be terrorized, so it was just another well-learned, planned step in the process.

There was a little group standing a short distance from the soldiers and their cross and game. There was Mary Magdalene, quiet with her memories. There was Mary, the wife of Clopas, someone we don't know much about. She is here because of the third woman, who was her sister. The third woman stood there, arms at her side, her eyes unmoving from the man on that cross. Her thoughts raced back to the well in Nazareth and the angel. She remembered Bethlehem and Egypt, and so many other things. Her son — whatever else that man on the cross may be, or may become — in her eyes at this moment in time, he is her son. No more, no less.

Jesus' eyes connected with hers for one very brief moment, as he said, "It is finished."

Easter Sunday
John 20:1-18

Early on the first day of the week, while it was still dark, Mary Magdalene came to the tomb and saw that the stone had been removed from the tomb. So she ran and went to Simon Peter and the other disciple, the one whom Jesus loved, and said to them, "They have taken the Lord out of the tomb, and we do not know where they have laid him." Then Peter and the other disciple set out and went toward the tomb. The two were running together, but the other disciple outran Peter and reached the tomb first. He bent down to look in and saw the linen wrappings lying there, but he did not go in. Then Simon Peter came, following him, and went into the tomb. He saw the linen wrappings lying there, and the cloth that had been on Jesus' head, not lying with the linen wrappings but rolled up in a place by itself. Then the other disciple, who reached the tomb first, also went in, and he saw and believed; for as yet they did not understand the scripture, that he must rise from the dead. Then the disciples returned to their homes. But Mary stood weeping outside the tomb. As she wept, she bent over to look into the tomb; and she saw two angels in white, sitting where the body of Jesus had been lying, one at the head and the other at the feet. They said to her, "Woman, why are you weeping?" She said to them, "They have taken away my Lord, and I do not know where they have laid him." When she had said this, she turned around and saw Jesus standing there, but she did not know that it was Jesus. Jesus said to her, "Woman, why are you weeping? Whom are you looking for?" Supposing him to be the gardener, she said to him, "Sir, if you have carried him away, tell me where you have laid him, and I will take him away." Jesus said to her, "Mary!" She turned and said to him in Hebrew, "Rabbouni!" (which means Teacher). Jesus said to her, "Do not hold on to me, because I have not yet ascended to the Father. But go to my brothers and say to them, 'I am ascending to my Father and your Father, to my God and your God.'" Mary Magdalene went and announced to the disciples, "I have seen the Lord"; and she told them that he had said these things to her.

Have You Ever Screwed Up?

Have you ever screwed up? I mean, really, really screwed up? It may have been fully well-intentioned or not, but the simple fact is that you knew you screwed up and so did everyone else. If you have, then you may have a slight idea of what the mood was in that little group of people who walked down the road that morning.

Only a few of them had actually been there to see what had happened on Friday; the rest had already run away or gone into hiding. As many times as those few told the story of what they had seen, no one could make sense of it. They spent the entire sabbath day talking together, trying to answer two questions.

First, what had gone wrong? For the past three years they had heard Jesus talking about a future that was bright and good, a future where everyone would be valued and every person would be treated as a child of God. Just last week, they came into Jerusalem with lots of followers and big celebrations, certain that what Jesus had been saying was about to become reality. But… what happened? Was Jesus wrong? Was he just another persuasive rebel who was able to brainwash them into following and believing? Were they all really that gullible? What had happened? And why did Judas do what he did? Did he somehow believe that if he forced a confrontation, Jesus would call down the angels from heaven right then and there? Or was he just a con artist? Why had it ended like this? What had happened to the kingdom? What happened to the dream? What had happened?

But it was the second question in each of their minds that was the more difficult and painful to answer. They realized that they may never understand "why" things turned out as they had, but they also realized that they would have to find the answer to this second question: *What do I do now?*

Matthew tried to answer that question. He closed his eyes and clearly pictured the day when he had pushed himself back from his desk, stood up, and walked out the office door, never to return. Being a tax collector had made him a powerful man, well-connected and wealthy as well. He had learned to live with the way the "normal people" hated him, but he didn't need to spend much time with the normal people anyway. He also still saw the looks on the faces of his former colleagues each time they saw him walking through town with this group of disciples over the next few years. He had become a joke to them. Not only had he walked away from their power and riches but he and his group actually argued against the very things that made them powerful and rich. How could he go back there again? Especially the way things had actually worked out; how could he ever again go home and have them look at him as anything other than a fool? Where would he go? What would he do?

Peter and the other fishermen had the same thoughts. How could they return to Bethsaida and Capernaum and face anyone? The brothers had walked away from the business they owned and were responsible for, not to mention leaving their wives and children. How many lives had they disrupted when they walked down the beach following this prophet? The prophet had now gone off and left them. For the first few months, whenever they would travel through town, their families would come out and stand on the street to greet them, tell them how much they missed them, and ask when they were coming back home. The elderly father they had left to run the business would look with hopeful eyes to see if they had come back to take the burden from his shoulders once again. But as the months went by, they stopped coming out and they stopped looking. How could any of these guys go back home and explain anything? Where would they go? What would they do?

Mary may have struggled the most with this question. If anyone was facing a difficult time returning home, it was this young woman from Magdala, the little town on the western shore of the Sea of Galilee. Scripture tells us she was a woman who was afflicted by seven demons that Jesus cast out.

Mary was a woman who had fallen under the prey of those seven demons; something not of her choosing. Unfortunately for her, it really made no difference. The common view was that if someone suffered for any reason, it was because they deserved it for some reason. And someone who was possessed by as many as seven demons, well, they clearly had done something quite serious and therefore should be avoided by the rest of the community. So people laughed and children threw stones.

Jesus and his little group had offered her a life she never had at home. For the past three years she was treated as a human being, felt valued, and actually began to believe that she was a child of God. Back in Magdala, on top of already being the outcast, she was now the one who had run off to follow the crazy preacher who got himself killed; proving her foolishness. So, where would she go? What would she do?

Perhaps that's why Mary was the first to get up this morning and make her way to the tomb. She was there to perform one final act of kindness to the one person who had treated her with any kind of love. That final act was to complete the formal burial ritual by cleaning the body, anointing it with sweet smelling oils, and then wrapping it in the formal burial cloth. This was usually done by family, and to Mary, this man was the only true family she knew.

The pain she was already feeling was compounded when she found that the tomb was opened, and the body was gone.

Not only had they taken away the hope she'd nurtured during the last three years, but now someone had taken away the chance for the one final act of love she had to offer. She ran back to Peter and another disciple with him, telling them what had happened. We can see the footrace that followed as the three of them all ran to the tomb. Peter was the last to get there, perhaps because he had already given up the hope needed for a good, fast run. Over the next few minutes, they walked in and out of the tomb, seeing the strips of burial cloth and the things Mary had brought for the anointing, but nothing else. I try to imagine the confusion in their minds as they slowly turned and walked away to go... somewhere.

Mary was the only one who stayed behind. It wasn't because she expected anything to happen. She just honestly did not know where else to go. She was as empty inside herself as was the tomb. The tears came. She was a strong woman and had stood up to the laughter and the stones. She had never bowed her head or wept. In her new life she had traveled the length of the country, holding her head up high as a follower of Jesus of Nazareth, believing his message about the value of all people. Now all that was left were the tears.

We know what happened next. It's one of the main reasons we are here this morning. Each gospel writer describes it differently, but in the next few minutes Mary is reminded that we can never assume we know what God is going to do. She and the other disciples had it all figured out, because it was something that was known. When someone died, they were buried and someone would perform the anointing ritual and it would then be over. Those left behind would have to fend for themselves and face on their own whatever was to come. Any dreams that had existed would cease to exist. That was how death worked. But in the next few minutes, Mary learned that we can never assume we understand God, and we can never define what God is going to be and do. Any time we attempt to put God in a box and begin to create rules that are intended to limit freedom and life, we're going to find that box empty. God does not stay in tombs or boxes. Anytime we try to limit God's love, God will pop up somewhere to let us know that our limits just don't stand.

My favorite image of Easter morning is not the empty tomb. As grand as that is, my favorite image of Easter morning is Mary's face... covered with beads of perspiration as she raced through the streets heading back to find Peter and the others. It is the look in her eyes as she thinks about how she will tell them that it is not over; they do not have to go back to the way things were. They hadn't screwed up after all.

It is not over!

Easter 2
John 20:19-31

When it was evening on that day, the first day of the week, and the doors of the house where the disciples had met were locked for fear of the Jews, Jesus came and stood among them and said, "Peace be with you." After he said this, he showed them his hands and his side. Then the disciples rejoiced when they saw the Lord. Jesus said to them again, "Peace be with you. As the Father has sent me, so I send you." When he had said this, he breathed on them and said to them, "Receive the Holy Spirit. If you forgive the sins of any, they are forgiven them; if you retain the sins of any, they are retained." But Thomas (who was called the Twin), one of the twelve, was not with them when Jesus came. So the other disciples told him, "We have seen the Lord." But he said to them, "Unless I see the mark of the nails in his hands, and put my finger in the mark of the nails and my hand in his side, I will not believe." A week later his disciples were again in the house, and Thomas was with them. Although the doors were shut, Jesus came and stood among them and said, "Peace be with you." Then he said to Thomas, "Put your finger here and see my hands. Reach out your hand and put it in my side. Do not doubt but believe." Thomas answered him, "My Lord and my God!" Jesus said to him, "Have you believed because you have seen me? Blessed are those who have not seen and yet have come to believe." Now Jesus did many other signs in the presence of his disciples, which are not written in this book. But these are written so that you may come to believe that Jesus is the Messiah, the Son of God, and that through believing you may have life in his name.

Uncertain Certainties

It was Sunday evening. Easter morning had come and gone, and the disciples had spent the entire day talking about the fact that Jesus had actually been raised from the dead. They were all fired up and making plans for how they were going to go out and spread the word of God and continue the ministry that Jesus had taught them to perform. Right?

Not quite.

As the sun went down Sunday evening, some of the disciples had gathered together. They were still hiding in a small room somewhere with the doors and windows closed and locked. Easter morning had come, but the disciples were still hiding, still overwhelmed by what happened at the end of the week, and still afraid that they might be the next ones to be arrested and killed. We can't really blame them, can we? I mean, even with the stories being told by Mary, Peter, and a few others about what they saw at the tomb that morning, it was all still just pretty overwhelming to make sense of wasn't it? What was about to happen next made things much more clear for them, but it really clouds everything more for us at the same time.

As they were huddled in their secure little hiding place, still filled with doubts and questions, we are told that Jesus came and stood among them. Over the next few minutes, their paralyzing fears were beginning to be transformed into the belief and confidence they would use to unlock the doors and windows and go out into the streets to change the world. It would be a few more weeks before they were fully ready to do that, but it began here.

All except for one guy. His name was Thomas.

Thomas was not with the group that Sunday evening. He was probably hiding in a place all of his own to avoid being caught with the others. When Thomas was told about Jesus appearing to the others in that closed room, his first response was more like ours.

"What? I don't believe it. I need some proof."

We're not told how the others responded to Thomas. We don't know if they gave him a hard time for not believing them, or if they accused him of not having enough faith. All we know is that the following week when they got together in that locked room, Thomas was there with them. We're told that Jesus appeared, walked over to Thomas and said, "Go ahead... touch me." Thomas asked for proof, and he got proof. Jesus talked with them a bit more and then said, "Have you believed because you have seen me? Blessed are those who have not seen and yet have come to believe." And then he left.

It's a bit unfair that this disciple ended up being known from then on as Doubting Thomas. I doubt he was any more doubtful than most of us are at times. To fault him for his doubts just doesn't seem fair at all. I probably would have said the same thing if it was me hearing that wild story. And being really honest, I sometimes wonder why old Thomas was able to get the proof he asked for, while some of us keep asking and asking for any kind of proof, and we still haven't seen anything yet. That's the key issue in this story, isn't it? That's the question that comes up any time we hear this story again. Sure, we're happy to see Thomas come around, but really, why is it that Jesus showed up then but doesn't pop in around here once in a while and give us a bit of proof too?

Please understand, I'm not making light of what happened in that closed room, and I'm not making light of the pain so many of us feel at times because of our very real doubts. It's just that I've seen so many people who are going through so many horrendously painful experiences. And I know that one little visit from Jesus, holding out his hand and saying "Put your finger here," would have made a huge difference to them and to those around them. It's only natural to ask, "Why doesn't he come? He came back for Thomas and the others, why not for us?"

I know people who have walked away from their faith because of this question. They asked questions like, "What kind of a God has the ability to show up and help people but chooses not to do that?" If Jesus could show up then, why not now?

And I've heard all kinds of answers.

I've been told that it is a test of our faith. I find it hard to believe that the God Jesus spoke of and prayed to as Daddy would allow the kinds of pain and suffering we see and consider it a "test."

I've been told that Jesus appeared to the first disciples to give them proof of his resurrection, and then gave them the responsibility to pass that message along to everyone else. John even ended today's passage by saying that the reason this story was written was "so that you may come to believe." The idea is that he passed responsibility for sharing the message to his followers, and it was then up to them to show others that Jesus was still around. This approach is helped along when we see the things that happened on Pentecost. The disciples received the additional help of God's Spirit to make their point. Perhaps so, but it would still be really helpful for a lot of us if we could just have one little piece of the kind of solid proof that Thomas got.

And I've been told that it is a simple matter of faith and not something we should even question. We simply have to believe. We should never question God because it demonstrates that we don't trust God, which shows that our faith is not strong. I have great respect for those people who can make that kind of a leap of faith, and who don't appear to have any questions or doubts hiding somewhere in the deep recesses of their mind and hearts. Unfortunately, I'm not one of those people. I have a lot of questions I would love to ask God, and I don't see that as an indication of any lack of faith. I recall many stories of God standing up to all kinds of questioning throughout the Bible. While the answers weren't always the ones the people were looking for, the questioners were not seen as bad for having asked the questions.

There is another possible way to explain why God has not always offered us the same proof that was offered to Thomas that Sunday evening in Jerusalem. Could it be that the reason God does not just give us that clear and unquestionable proof we keep asking for is that it might actually create more harm for us than help? As crazy as it sounds, is it actually possible that life might be more difficult and painful if we really had that *proof* that God was real and that Jesus actually did come back to life on that Easter morning? Is it just possible that we would actually be happier, and more alive, if we never had that proof we want?

I can think of a few reasons this might be the case. First, imagine that right here, right now, God appeared in front of us and in that nice, deep voice, said, "Yes, it's all true." Our first reaction might be some pretty awesome amazement and a brief and deep sigh of relief as we have our deepest questions answered once and for all. But then, maybe after only a few minutes, it would begin to sink in: What do we do now? There is no more room for doubt, no more room for those theological discussions about good and evil, right and wrong, and for philosophizing about the purpose of life. All of that is answered by this one appearance. The only thing left for us to do now is either to obey or not obey. God's appearance proves once and for all that Jesus was telling the truth when he said that the one, single commandment we are to follow is to love one another — period. And, remember, he was talking about that kind of love that gives away shoes, coats, and money. The kind of love that shares the dining room table with people you can't even stand to be around. The kind of love that ended up getting Jesus killed. If we knew for certain this was the way we were to behave, we would either obey that one commandment, or we would not obey. Are we really sure we want that kind of clarity?

And there would be other issues coming up soon after we got over the initial shock of seeing God standing here in the room. After all, we're made of the same stuff as the disciples, with the same human passions. After a few minutes there would probably be some gentle pushing and shoving as we all tried to get just a bit closer to where God was standing. There might be some minor bickering over who got to stand the closest. Would it be decided by age or should we run to the office and get a copy of the spreadsheet to see who has given more to support God's church, and line up according to that ranking? People would start shouting out other questions they would really like to have answers for concerning major life decisions, why something happened as it did and… what Wednesday's Lotto numbers would be!

Within a few minutes someone would send a tweet, and the parking lot would fill with people from the media, setting up satellite dishes and shoving microphones into everyone's face. My guess is that God would not stick around for that circus, so it would be up to us to explain it all, trying not to sound too crazy in the process. The other churches around would have problems with the whole idea, demanding to know why God would show up for us instead of at their place of worship. Non-Christians around the world would challenge us, perhaps accusing us of trying to discredit their beliefs and traditions, many of which have been around much longer than ours. Again, even if none of those sillier things actually happened, if God did actually appear to us here this morning, all of us with lunch warming in the oven, or reservations made at the restaurant, with warm coats and dry shoes, all of us would be faced with the decision whether or not we were going to give those away to see that the hungry are fed, and the cold are clothed. If we had solid proof that our number one command was to love one another we would have to make decisions.

Okay, I'm having a little fun with the idea, but honestly, the more you think about it, the less of a good idea it seems to be to have God suddenly show up and give us the proof we want.

If God showed up here this morning and walked up to each one of us here and said, "Go ahead, touch me," what would happen to our faith? Oh, we would have the proof we wanted but we would then only have to make a cold and rational choice to obey or not obey. And that choice would not be based on anything inside of us but upon the logical reality that if we didn't obey, we were clearly in the wrong. The decision to obey God would not be something we felt, or something based on who we really are inside, but a simple, mechanical act of compliance, a step taken to ensure we are going to be okay. We might not really feel like loving each other, but if that's what we have to do, well, we'll do what we have to do. Like the child of the over-controlling parent or the employee of the micromanaging boss, we will do what we have to do to get by but it will never be something we truly cared about.

The great gift of being asked to live by faith is that we have the freedom of choice. This is the blessing Jesus was talking about after meeting Thomas. As lucky as Thomas was to have his proof, he actually lost something in that process. This is something that God considers to be a greater treasure than proof — the treasure of choice.

Choice was important enough to God to give it to the very first humans, even if it meant the risk of them making a poor choice in the process. Abraham was given choices, as were Jacob, Moses, and every other leader of the faith throughout history. Even Jesus was given choice, as we remember his final prayer in Gethsemane, when he finally said, "Okay, Dad, I'll stay and go through with this." It is choice that God offers as blessing.

There are those today who fear choice, especially when it is related to one's personal lives and religious beliefs. They feel a responsibility, not to prove anything to us because they have no more real answers than the rest of us have, but they believe they are correct to try and force us to believe in and to obey their views, by intimidation, by manipulation through power, or by clear and simple murder. To this group, questioning is wrong. Thinking is wrong. Allowing choice is wrong. What they offer is not a life of faith, but a life of blind obedience no different than the obedience demanded by Annas and Pilate as they spoke with Jesus during his trial. They are demanding obedience to something that Jesus gave his life to fight against.

Without human choice, and without the uncertain certainties of faith, we simply obey and do what we are told, whether we mean it or not. It is empty. It has nothing to do with love or trust. When we stand here in the middle of our doubts and questions and we look around at everything happening around us that creates such pain and inequality as we see in the world, when we live in that world and we can still look at this God and his Son and say, "I choose to believe in you," that is the blessing. The wonderful thing about choice is that when we make it, it is because it is based on what we believe inside, in our hearts and minds. It is a true act that reflects who we are and not something we do because we have to. It is the act of intentional love that we have chosen to base our lives around. It can never be shaken by questions or doubts, because it does not rely upon that type of proof.

Ask your questions, voice your doubts, and choose to believe in spite of them all.

"Blessed are those who have not seen me and yet have come to believe" (v. 29).

Easter 3
Luke 24:36b-48

While they were talking about this, Jesus himself stood among them and said to them, "Peace be with you." They were startled and terrified, and thought that they were seeing a ghost. He said to them, "Why are you frightened, and why do doubts arise in your hearts? Look at my hands and my feet; see that it is I myself. Touch me and see; for a ghost does not have flesh and bones as you see that I have." And when he had said this, he showed them his hands and his feet. While in their joy they were disbelieving and still wondering, he said to them, "Have you anything here to eat?" They gave him a piece of broiled fish, and he took it and ate in their presence. Then he said to them, "These are my words that I spoke to you while I was still with you — that everything written about me in the law of Moses, the prophets, and the psalms must be fulfilled." Then he opened their minds to understand the scriptures, and he said to them, "Thus it is written, that the Messiah is to suffer and to rise from the dead on the third day, and that repentance and forgiveness of sins is to be proclaimed in his name to all nations, beginning from Jerusalem. You are witnesses of these things."

Fish Tales

Have you ever had to sell an idea or a concept or a belief? Have you ever had to sell something intangible, something you couldn't see, touch, or taste? And maybe it was an idea that was really rather strange; one that most people would find really hard to believe. So, before you actually got someone to believe in the idea, you first have to somehow convince them that the idea is even possible.

What if you weren't trying to sell this idea because it was a part of your job or even something you were being paid to sell? What if you were trying to sell this idea because God had appeared to you and told you to sell it? What if you woke up in the middle of the night, because God was standing at the foot of your bed tugging on your toe? You woke up, and God looked at you and said, "I want you to convince everyone that this idea is true! In fact, I'm making it your responsibility to sell it to them." You would have no choice.

You get the idea. Have you ever really needed to convince someone of something that was really difficult to convince them of? That is the problem the guy is faced with in the passage from Luke today. The writer of Luke's gospel was faced with a huge challenge as he wrote his version of the story of Jesus.

God always provided guidance and direction for those individuals who were selected to do important things. Abraham, Moses, David, Solomon; there is a long list of people who had God's guidance as they did their part in the history of our faith. However, it is also important to remember that for each one of those people, they still ended up having to do a lot of the hard work themselves. God certainly provided direction, but the people still invested their blood, sweat, and tears as they tried to understand just how to get the job done. Just because God provides guidance and direction, it does not mean that we get to sit back and watch things happen all on their own. Our writer certainly had direction from God but that did not mean he got to sit back and watch the words write themselves.

I can see Luke sitting at his desk, forehead leaning on his hand, staring at the piece of parchment trying to figure out how to say what he needed to say to sell the idea he had to sell. Maybe he had been there a while. There was a pile of crumpled-up parchment pages scattered on the floor. Anyone who has written something difficult knows the experience he was having sitting there.

But Luke had an advantage that many writers do not have. Someone had already taken a shot at writing the story he had to write, trying to sell the same idea he had to sell. He actually had Mark's copy of the story there on the desk with him, and he copied pieces from it to help with his own version of the story. At that time, copying from another writer was not seen as a bad thing but was a way to use the earlier writer's thoughts to help make your own point. Mark had written his version for a very different audience than the one for whom Luke was writing. Mark wrote in the simple version of Greek used by the common people, since those were the people to whom he was trying to talk. Luke, however, was trying to tell the story to a different type of reader. That was the main problem he was having. His audience was a tough one.

While Mark wrote to the common folks, Luke had the task of telling his version of the story to the upper-crust folks of the cities of Antioch and Rome. These were not only more educated people, who asked lots of questions the common folks just didn't care about. Luke was writing to people who were already very religious, and who were already people of faith in their own way. While Mark's crowd might be impressed with the basic stories, Luke's audience was not. Miracles? Yeah, our gods do that. Life after death? Sure, we got that. No big deal.

The early disciples saw the resurrection as one of the most powerful pieces of their story, and as the early church grew, the resurrection was a central message. But it was not a new idea in either Antioch or Rome. The idea of life after death was commonplace in most religions, and there was quite a variety of different approaches to the idea. As these folks read Mark's story of the resurrection of Jesus, their response was, "Yeah, okay. That's kind of like Uncle Fred, when his spirit came back at the temple of Zeus." The idea of returning spirits was commonplace, and there was a very detailed list of the various types of life-after-death experiences that took place. There were spirits, which were sometimes only voices or faint visions of the person. There were ghosts, which looked real enough to be the person, but if you tried to touch them your hand would pass right through them. They did not have any real substance. There were several other categories, but the one primary rule that applied to them all was that they were not real and they did not eat. Think about it. If they had no real substance, where would the food go after they ate it? The fact that Jesus came back to life was just fine with these folks but there was no reason whatsoever to think he was any different than Uncle Fred, and certainly no reason to convert to some new religion based on that story alone.

Luke sat there with all of this running through his mind. Then it struck him and he began to write. He began the story innocently enough, simply telling one of the other stories that Mark chose not to tell.

It was Sunday afternoon, the same day that Mary and others found the tomb was empty. Two of the disciples had made the seven-mile walk to Emmaus. Luke doesn't tell us who they were or why they went to the little town of Emmaus because that's not why he was telling the story; it just was not important to him. While the two were walking, they ran into a stranger on the road and were surprised to find that he had not heard anything about what had happened earlier that morning at the tomb. They were even more surprised when they found out later that this stranger was actually Jesus, giving them the same greeting he would give the others in that closed room later on. Luke was sparse on some details, again because this is not the reason he was telling the story. We're still just reading the prologue here.

After returning from Emmaus, the two disciples were with some of the others, telling them about the experience they just had with the stranger, who turned out to be Jesus. We were told they still weren't really convinced, but before we have time to think much more about that, Luke tells us that Jesus appeared again, right in the middle of their story-telling. This was where Luke began to make his point.

Jesus greeted them as he did in other appearances and tried to calm their startled nerves. Luke shares the part of the story that Mark omitted, which was going to change the entire story for his audience.

After the greeting, Jesus realized they thought they were seeing a ghost. So he said, "Touch me and see; for a ghost does not have flesh and bones as you see that I have" (v. 39). Luke's readers pause at this point and take notice.

Jesus then said, "Have you anything here to eat?" (v. 41). They handed him a piece of broiled fish. He ate it.

Jesus then went on to teach the disciples as he did each time he appeared to them, and said some things that were important. However, Luke's readers will have to come back and read those things later, because at this point they are stumped: "He ate the fish? How did he eat the fish?"

That was why Luke wrote his gospel. It was simply one, long fish tale. All of the rest is important, yes. Even here at this point, Jesus tells the disciples that his death was for a purpose. He says that repentance and forgiveness are available for everyone and they are witnesses to it all. Because of that, they have a responsibility to share the story.

Does it sound silly to say that the main reason Luke wrote his gospel was because ghosts can't eat fish? Yes, perhaps it does today. But as Luke wrote it, he was simply trying to figure out how to tell the story in a way that made the most sense to the people he was trying to convince. He didn't make things up. He thought about what was the most important to his audience, and he wrote the story that focused on those things.

If something as silly as "Jesus ate fish!" had the impact it did for Luke's audience, I wonder what simple message would have the most impact on our audience today?

And I wonder if we have the courage to retell the story to speak that message?

Easter 4
John 10:11-18

I am the good shepherd. The good shepherd lays down his life for the sheep. The hired hand, who is not the shepherd and does not own the sheep, sees the wolf coming and leaves the sheep and runs away — and the wolf snatches them and scatters them. The hired hand runs away because a hired hand does not care for the sheep. I am the good shepherd. I know my own and my own know me, just as the Father knows me and I know the Father. And I lay down my life for the sheep. I have other sheep that do not belong to this fold. I must bring them also, and they will listen to my voice. So there will be one flock, one shepherd. For this reason the Father loves me, because I lay down my life in order to take it up again. No one takes it from me, but I lay it down of my own accord. I have power to lay it down, and I have power to take it up again. I have received this command from my Father.

The Shepherd

He woke up just as the sun was peeking over the top of the mountains to the east, just as he had done every morning for the past couple of months. He took a few minutes to enjoy the beauty of it all, and then quickly got up and took a quick look in every direction to make sure everything was safe. He made one quick trip around the low, stone wall of the sheepfold, making sure the wall was still secure. Then he stopped at the gap in the wall filled with briars, at the gate. The sheep began to stir as he walked around, and one by one they walked over to the gate to begin the day.

With all sheep accounted for after a safe night, his first task was to see that they all had a good drink of water. He had planned this last night, so he knew the direction to lead them that would be the safest to take. He knew that there was really no such thing as a "safe" path in this country. That's why he had the sling hung on his belt and the small leather pouch filled with stones. The sling and stone was not just used to slay giants, as David once did. They were also quite effective against things like mountain lions. And, like all other experienced shepherds, he was a crack shot with his sling.

He also carried his crook, the long stick with the curved hook on the end. It wasn't just for show, nor was it some kind of a badge to let everyone know he was a shepherd. The stick was a perfect second line of defense against any intruder, like a wild animal or a thief, determined to steal a sheep or two. A quick, firm thump on the head with that solid piece of wood would quickly convince any attacker to look someplace else.

And the hook? There were many times that, to get his flock from one place to another, the shepherd had to lead them along some fairly difficult paths. Some of them went through dangerous forests where the wild animals hid so well. Some of them went up and down through really steep and dangerous canyons with trails that had sharp cliffs on both sides. Once in a while, one of the sheep would miss a step and fall from the path. This happened a lot on one of the trails the shepherds used a lot, leading from the dry lands around Jericho to the green pasture lands up near Bethlehem and Jerusalem. That trail went through a valley that was dangerous, filled with wild animals, thieves, and steep, narrow paths. The valley was called "the Shadow of Death." As careful as they were, sometimes a sheep would lose its footing on that dangerous path and fall from the trail into the ravines. The shepherd would take his staff, and using the long pole like a fishhook, would reach down into the crevice, reach the hook around the leg of the poor sheep, and gently lift him back up onto the trail. As he led his flock toward the water, he was hoping to avoid those kinds of nasty surprises.

Last night before he went to sleep, he had walked around to find the safest path to lead his flock to the water. Not only was it important to find the safest path but he had to be very careful to find the right watering hole as well. His sheep did not swim well, especially now that their woolly coats were filling out so well. If they fell into the water, they would soak it up like a sponge, and he might not be able to pull them back out, even with his sturdy hooked staff. He had to search around to find quiet waters, a place where the currents were still, where they could safely drink with no risk of being caught and pulled away. He knew this land very well, including the perfect watering spot, right next to a very nice pasture where his sheep could graze today. After planning his path last night, he was ready to lead them there this morning.

While his sheep enjoyed their morning drinks, the shepherd walked around the nearby pasture. He walked slowly, closely examining every inch of ground. He stopped to pick up any sharp stones or briars that might cut the soft noses of his sheep. He looked for those plants that might be poisonous or that might cause illness. He looked for scorpions, snakes, or insect nests that might harm his flock as they innocently grazed in this place. There were enemies everywhere, and it was his responsibility to prepare their dinner table, right in the middle of all of them.

After they had their fill of water, the sheep began to move to the pasture and settle in for their normal day of doing what sheep do. The shepherd found a tree nearby where he could see the entire pasture and settled down in the shade, keeping one eye alert for any danger to his flock.

One of the things he was watching for was to make sure none of the sheep wandered away from the flock and got lost. Sometimes, a sheep might find a really great patch of food, and with her head down, just keep eating and walking until she'd have followed the path away from the rest of the flock. If that single sheep got far enough away from the shepherd with his sling and staff, it became the perfect victim for enemies hiding nearby. When the shepherd found that one of his sheep was missing, his one goal was to find that lost sheep. The rest of the flock were relatively safe together, so the shepherd focused on finding the lost one. Any shepherd worth his salt would search until that lost sheep was found. Fortunately today, he found it just over the hill and quickly guided it back to the safety of the flock.

Once in a while, the shepherd might find a sheep that belonged to someone else, one that had wandered off. In that case, he took that sheep into his own fold and cared for it as it if were his own, until he could find the sheep's true owner.

Any lost sheep was welcomed into his fold. No sheep was left to stand alone and risk the dangers of not being a part of the flock.

None of these sheep were actually his. It was quite common that shepherds did not own any sheep of their own. Some did, but they were rare. Most shepherds spent their time taking care of sheep that belonged to someone else. At the beginning of grazing season, the shepherd would travel from place to place, collecting the sheep that were being entrusted to him. He would then lead them to the grazing lands where he would be responsible for them until safely returning them to their masters several weeks or months later. They would return healthy and covered in valuable wool, and the shepherd would receive his reward for all of his hard work. If he lost any sheep, he would have to pay for them out of his reward. More importantly, the shepherd who lost sheep would soon be seen as untrustworthy and would quickly find himself without any owners willing to hire him.

Protecting the sheep was more than just a financial issue for the shepherd. The shepherd who did not protect his flock was not a shepherd. He might be considered a hired hand, someone who was paid to do something and who may or may not do it very well. But if he truly wanted to be a shepherd, his number one responsibility was to take care of each and every one of the sheep that was entrusted to his care — even if that meant risking his own life to protect them. Even if it meant placing himself, his sling, and his staff between his flock and an attacking mountain lion or band of thieves. If he did not protect his flock, he was not a shepherd.

There were no highly visible, great rewards for being a shepherd. The pay was fine but it was not enough with which to build a comfortable home. Besides, since he was out taking care of someone else's sheep for months at a time, taking care of a nice home of their own was just not feasible for most shepherds. It wasn't a job that earned high levels of respect in the community, other than from sheep owners and other shepherds. Most shepherds were really good with sheep but not always all that good with people. That's probably why they enjoyed spending so much time out on their own, up in the hills, away from the rest of the community. Shepherds were always there, a part of the community but never really one of those groups. Shepherds were merely seen as a group of people who took care of someone else's sheep.

As our shepherd sat under his shade tree, an interesting thing happened. Throughout the day, one by one, each sheep would move apart from the flock and walk over to stand next to the shepherd. He would quietly talk with them, scratch their ear or rub their belly; he knew what each of them liked. After a few minutes of attention, the sheep would then return to the flock and continue their day. The sheep knew their shepherd's voice and could tell his voice apart from that of other shepherds. Even in the confusion that happened when two flocks happened to meet on the same trail, the sheep knew their shepherd's voice and could easily follow him. He was their shepherd.

As the sun began to fade in late afternoon, the shepherd led the flock back to the still waters again, and then back to the stone sheepfold. As the sheep lined up to enter the narrow gate, the shepherd knelt down and examined each of them as they entered, one by one. He called them by name and rubbed some healing oil on any cuts or scrapes they might have gotten on their soft noses during the day. After each sheep was safely inside the fold, the shepherd piled the briars up tightly at the entrance to form the secure gate. He then walked all around the sheepfold, securing any loose stones, and stacking more briars on top of the wall where it might be needed to discourage any predators from trying to jump the wall. Only then, after seeing that his flock was safe for the night, did the shepherd find his comfortable spot in the little stone tower he had built nearby, and settle in for the night.

As through the day, he spends the night with one eye resting, while the other keeps a sharp look for anything that might threaten his sheep. It is just what he did.

When the sun came up on this particular morning, it was different. It was the end of the grazing season, and after checking each of his sheep, he led them from the waters, back down the long trail toward the city. One by one, he presented each sheep to their owners, until he had safely returned each and every sheep that had been entrusted to him. He felt the weight of the pouch he carried, now filled with the coins from his payment for the past months' work. But more than that, he felt a warmth inside knowing he had done what he had set out to do. He had taken care of each and every one of his sheep. He was no hired hand. He was a shepherd.

As he made his way back to his humble home, he noticed the group of people standing down by the sea. They were standing and sitting along the shore, all listening to one guy who was talking with them. As he walked nearer, he remembered things he had heard about this man — this teacher. As a shepherd, he really didn't know or care much for things like prophets and miracle workers. His main concern was his sheep. Don't misunderstand, he was a man of faith. You had to have a strong faith to stand in front of real danger holding only a sling and a stick, but his faith was not the sort you spent a lot of time talking about and debating. You either stood up to your enemies, or you didn't. It was a pretty basic faith.

He walked toward the back of the crowd, more out of curiosity than anything else. As he moved closer in order to be able to hear better, he suddenly found himself standing in the middle of a group of people who did not seem very happy to see him. They were dressed in stylish robes, covered in fine linens and jewels, and smelled like they had been doused in expensive perfumes. They were all looking at him with disdain. He was as clean as anyone could be who had spent the past months living in the mountains with sheep. But he had not been fortunate enough to have covered his body with expensive oils as these priests had, so in comparison, yes, perhaps he did stand out a bit from that crowd.

Perhaps it was the look they gave the shepherd, or the hesitance he saw in the shepherd's eyes that caught the speaker's attention. Whatever it was, it was at that point that Jesus looked right at them and said, "I am the good shepherd." As he looked directly at the poor shepherd, he went on to say things like "the good shepherd lays down his life for his sheep" (v. 11), "I know my own sheep, and my own know me" (v. 14), and "I lay down my life for my sheep" (v. 15).

His gaze switched to those nice-smelling priests when he said, "The hired hand, who is not the shepherd and does not own the sheep, sees the wolf coming and leaves the sheep and runs away," and "the hired hand does not care for the sheep" (vv. 12-13).

Every eye in the crowd was now on these two groups: the rich, powerful, perfumed priests, and this fresh-from-the-hills shepherd, just waiting to see what was going to happen next. It was clear that Jesus had struck a nerve somewhere. The earlier smiles and looks of self-satisfaction on the faces of the priests had changed to a look of raw anger, as though they were trying to figure out who they should destroy first: this little sheepherder or this rabble-rousing preacher.

Before they could make up their minds, Jesus pushed things further by saying, "So there will be one flock, one shepherd" (v. 16). Now he had the priests' full attention but they were no longer listening to what he said. They had already made up their minds. In a matter of seconds, Jesus had declared that the shepherd was of more value than the priest. The shepherd was trustworthy, and the priest was a hired hand.

And "one flock"? Never. Religious law was clear that there was a distinction between those who were clean and those who were unclean. There was not "one flock" and there never would be. *They* were the leaders of the true flock, and *they* had the power and authority behind them to make sure that it continued to be that way.

They looked at the shepherd and still saw him as harmless, meaningless, and of no real threat. The threat was in front of them. With the look of blood in their eyes, they glared at this preacher who now called himself the "good shepherd." He would have to go.

While all of this was burning through the minds of the priests, scribes, and Pharisees, the shepherd calmly moved back through the crowd, already thinking of the work he had to get done today. He had sheep to collect, to take back to the hills, and to care for. It is what the good shepherd does.

Easter 5
John 15:1-8

I am the true vine, and my Father is the vinegrower. He removes every branch in me that bears no fruit. Every branch that bears fruit he prunes to make it bear more fruit. You have already been cleansed by the word that I have spoken to you. Abide in me as I abide in you. Just as the branch cannot bear fruit by itself unless it abides in the vine, neither can you unless you abide in me. I am the vine, you are the branches. Those who abide in me and I in them bear much fruit, because apart from me you can do nothing. Whoever does not abide in me is thrown away like a branch and withers; such branches are gathered, thrown into the fire, and burned. If you abide in me, and my words abide in you, ask for whatever you wish, and it will be done for you. My Father is glorified by this, that you bear much fruit and become my disciples.

Tangled Up in the Vines

This passage from John is one that has created great comfort for many people, and at the same time has created profound pain and suffering for others. It has pulled us together and brutally split us apart. This simple story of a vine, growing in a vineyard, both heals and destroys. Many who read this story see it as a reason to turn away from the biblical story.

Let's begin by recognizing what was going on when Jesus first told this story of the vine. It will help us to remember that stories about a vine and vineyard have been told since ancient times, so it is not something new with Jesus.

The Old Testament prophets, Isaiah, Jeremiah, and Ezekiel, talked about vines and vineyards. It's important to remember that these prophets arose and spoke during times of great threat to the country. They spent their time warning the people what was going to happen to them if they did not behave. The prophets had an ability to say things in ways that people understood, and since most folks back then were familiar with vineyards, they got to the point quickly.

In chapter 5 of Isaiah, the prophet told a story about someone who built a beautiful vineyard on a fertile hill, doing everything needed to create an ideal setting for the vines. But the vineyard failed. The owner said, "When I expected it to yield domestic grapes, why did it yield wild grapes?" He then tore down the protective wall and hedge, let the vineyard become overgrown with briars, and commanded the clouds to stop raining on it. That last detail makes it clear that the owner being described was God, and the vineyard of wild grapes was the people of Israel. Isaiah used familiar language to make his point, attempting to call the nation back from the destruction that threatened them.

Later, Jeremiah told his listeners, "Yet I planted you as a choice vine, from the purest stock. How then did you degenerate and become a wild vine?" (Jeremiah 2:21). In Jeremiah's time, the word "wild" actually meant "foreign." So Jeremiah was using the familiar story to warn the people to stop worshiping foreign gods, and warning them what will happen if they do not stop.

Many years later, Ezekiel tells the nation, "Your mother was like a vine in a vineyard transplanted by the water, fruitful and full of branches from abundant water" (Ezekiel 19:12). The mother was the land of Judah, then under threat by Babylon. Because of the behavior of the people of Judah, it was "plucked up in fury, cast down to the ground; the east wind dried it up, its fruit was cut off." Ezekiel painted the picture that everyone understood. Unfortunately, they didn't listen to it.

Matthew told how Jesus used the vine and vineyard in a parable of how the vineyard owner's son was killed by those who were supposed to be taking care of the vineyard.

So as Jesus talked about the vine, the disciples would have put it in context with the long history of stories about vines and vineyards.

Jesus told this little story while he and the disciples were all gathered together after celebrating the Passover seder, and only a few minutes after Judas had bolted from the room as the traitor. If there was ever an opportunity to talk about wild grapes, this would have been it.

In the next few minutes, Jesus was either going to say something profoundly kind and loving, or something that is so brutal and harsh that it will end up dividing and destroying families and nations even today.

Jesus says, "I am the true vine" (v. 1).

Think of what goes through the disciples' minds immediately. For generations of vine stories, the vine has represented the true way, the true vision for what the people of Israel were meant to be. The vine has been God's way.

Jesus then began talking about pruning the vineyard, and this is where the problems began. Sounding very much like the doomsday prophets of old, Jesus said, "He removes every branch in me that bears no fruit" (v. 2). And he ends this with the statement that "whoever does not abide in me is thrown away like a branch and withers; such branches are gathered, thrown into the fire, and burned."

There we have it. Those few sentences have created voices that scream for active pruning away of those who do not seem to bear fruit, those who appear to be producing wild grapes. The passage is used as the commandment to separate ourselves from those who do not produce the fruit that is seen as being appropriate for our vineyard. While laws see to it that these people cannot literally be cast into the fire, it has still been possible to cast them out in other ways. They are banned. They are shunned. They are treated as though they no longer exist. They are seen as infidels, as sinful, or as unclean. It is important that we identify those people who are the "wild grapes," and that we cut them off from the vine so they do not corrupt the rest of the vineyard, isn't it? Isn't that what Jesus is clearly saying here?

And Jesus repeatedly used the word "abide" as he tells this story. "Whoever does not abide in me is thrown away," and "Those who abide in me and me in them bear much fruit" (v. 6). A quick search of the dictionary points out that there are two primary definitions for the word *abide*, one of which is "to withstand, tolerate, endure, or put up with." Isn't Jesus actually saying that while it may be difficult sometimes to take the harsh step of cutting some people out of the vineyard, if we withstand the pain and tolerate or endure the hurt that may come with it, we are doing his will by protecting the vineyard from the possible corruption from those who are wild grapes? Is that the real meaning?

While it is true that Jesus does say, more than once, the vines that do not produce fruit will be removed, it is important to note he never once suggests that it is *our* responsibility to do the pruning. Not once does Jesus even suggest that it is *our* role to judge the value of the vines. Not once. Jesus says, "He removes every branch…" and "Whoever does not abide in me is thrown away…" and "such branches are gathered…" (vv. 2, 6). Jesus is saying that while there may be some pruning of wild grapes done at some point, it is not *our* job. We are to leave that to the hand of the owner of the vineyard, the vine grower, the only one who has the ability to measure the value of any vine.

The other definition of the word *abide* is "to remain, to continue in relationship with, to dwell." It means more than to tolerate, or put up with. It means we believe in something enough to live with it. It is where we stay.

With that in mind, it may help us understand what Jesus is saying a bit better. Was Jesus saying that even if we don't like what he wants, we are supposed to tolerate him and just go along? That no longer makes sense after he says, "Abide in me as I abide in you."

The story of the vineyard and vine is a story of everyone being connected and together, rather than of cutting off and separating. It is when the parts of the vineyard are all connected that the good fruit is produced. All of the different parts of the vineyard: the soil, the roots, the vines, the leaves… as different as they are to look at, they each have their value in producing good fruit. If there are unfruitful branches, it is not our problem or our focus. Rather than trying to find those vines that need to be cut off, our only purpose is to work together to produce the fruit the vineyard owner planted us here to produce.

It's that simple.

Easter 6
John 15:9-17

As the Father has loved me, so I have loved you; abide in my love. If you keep my commandments, you will abide in my love, just as I have kept my Father's commandments and abide in his love. I have said these things to you so that my joy may be in you, and that your joy may be complete. "This is my commandment, that you love one another as I have loved you. No one has greater love than this, to lay down one's life for one's friends. You are my friends if you do what I command you. I do not call you servants any longer, because the servant does not know what the master is doing; but I have called you friends, because I have made known to you everything that I have heard from my Father. You did not choose me but I chose you. And I appointed you to go and bear fruit, fruit that will last, so that the Father will give you whatever you ask him in my name. I am giving you these commands so that you may love one another.

What a Friend

In your mind, I'd like you to picture a good friend. It may be a current friend or one from the past. Just take a moment, think of a good friend, and picture them in your mind's eye. Can you see them? When did you first meet them? How did they become a friend?

Let's leave your friend hanging around for a few minutes; we'll come back to them later. They are going to help us make sense of the scripture reading this morning.

The passage from John is describing some of the things Jesus said to his disciples as they sat around the Passover seder table, after the meal. He was taking this final opportunity to try to help the disciples understand what was about to happen and to help prepare them for the work they were going to have to do. This is one of those passages that has sometimes created some real confusion for those reading it. In fact, this one passage has caused many people to question their entire faith and has been the reason many people have lost their faith entirely. Let's take a look, and with a little help from our friend in our mind, see if we can clear up some of the problem.

Jesus was talking about his relationship with the men sitting around the table. Up to this point, the disciples had been in the role of learners, followers, perhaps even servants, following the teaching and direction that Jesus had given them. He began by explaining that everything he had been doing and talking about came down to love. Just as God has loved him, he has loved them. And now, the number one commandment they are to obey is to love one another. While this sounds nice to us, it would have been a bit more impressive to the guys at the table. There was a very long, long list of commandments for a first-century Jewish man to obey. They covered every possible part of life. Each commandment had points and sub-points and included a similar very long list of penalties for those who chose to disobey any particular commandment. The priests also had a long list of steps you had to go through to be forgiven for breaking a commandment, many of which involved a fairly large amount of money to be paid to the temple. Most people spent a significant part of their day trying very hard to not violate any commandments, because for many of them, it was nearly impossible to jump the hurdles necessary to obtain official forgiveness. And without forgiveness, a commandment breaker was seen as unclean, one who could not participate in normal daily activities. So these guys knew about commandments, most of which dealt with everything except love. Love was now the *one* commandment that counted. This would take some time to figure out.

Jesus complicated things even more by then explaining that, from this point on, by following this one commandment, the men around the table were no longer disciples or servants, but they were Jesus' *friends*. "I do not call you servants any longer, because the servant does not know what the master is doing; but I have called you friends" (v. 15). This was a huge promotion, a major change in the relationship between Jesus and the men at the table. He then said: "And I appointed you to go and bear fruit, fruit that will last, so that the Father will give you whatever you ask him in my name" (v. 16).

Wait a minute. God will give us anything we ask for if we ask for it in Jesus' name? Since we are no longer servants, but we are now Jesus' friends, he will do this for us? Really?

That's what John says.

But wait! If Jesus did say that God would give us anything we asked for if we asked for it in his name, then why doesn't it always work? I'm guessing there are a few of us here who have spoken some very sincere prayers at times, asking for something very important, like the end of an illness, the healing of an injury, the healing of a relationship, a new job, a decent meal. We've prayed these things sitting at a hospital bedside, in funeral homes, in rooms at home filled with the dark and quiet that comes after a painful argument, and while watching children who have no food, no bed — nothing.

Based on what John said, if our prayers haven't been answered, some would argue that it means we've not lived up to our part of the deal: to go out and bear fruit. But isn't that pretty subjective? What kind of fruit? And how much fruit? Some of us have spent a lifetime doing everything we can to bear fruit and love those around us; yet when we ask in Jesus' name, nothing happens. Some find an answer to this by creating a bunch of rules that have to be followed, promising that they will then result in enough fruit to get your prayers heard. But Jesus didn't say there were any other rules. Creating new rules is an attempt to find an excuse to explain why the things that John tells us in his writing don't always happen.

In plain and simple terms, if John says our prayers will be answered if we ask them in Jesus' name, why aren't they always answered? If Jesus is a friend, which is the basis for the whole thing, why doesn't he act like a true friend and keep his promise?

I understand that may sound harsh and something that some might consider inappropriate to hear from a pulpit. But it is a question we have asked many times, and in many cases, it is the question that breaks our faith. God made a promise to answer our prayers, but does not always keep it. What kind of a loving God does that?

Some argue that God does answer every one of our prayers. However, sometimes God answers them in ways we don't understand, because sometimes God knows there is a better answer than the one we are after. But those experiencing the pain of unanswered prayer might say that's not what Jesus said. It was pretty clear, wasn't it? John wrote: "And I appointed you to go and bear fruit, fruit that will last, so that the Father will give you whatever you ask him in my name" (v. 16). It doesn't say, "Unless God has a better answer."

Again, what kind of friend makes a promise like that and refuses to keep it?

To see if we can ease the pain, let's go back to the beginning and look at the friend you brought into memory when we first started. When I asked you to get an image in mind of your friend, the chances are very good that we actually pictured two different types of friends. This is an important thing to understand, and it may help us as we look again at that promise John tells us that Jesus made.

For some of us, the friend we saw in front of us was someone who was very close to us. There was an intimacy between the two of you, a level of trust and respect that helped you share things you would not be able to share with others. It was someone with whom you spent a lot of time, and even when you were not together, there was something between you that kept the two of you near in your thoughts. This friend became a real part of your life, and in a very real sense, life would just not be the same without them. This friend was a buddy, a pal, an equal with you who shared their lives with you as you shared yours with them. This was a friend who kept promises they made with you, unless it was physically impossible to do. Even then, they did something — they came as close to fulfilling the promise as they could.

Picturing Jesus as this type of friend leads to the problem we find in John's writing. A true friend would never make a promise that was so vague and difficult to understand, and then not even honor it when we really, really needed them to do so.

But there is another definition of the word friend, and some here may be picturing someone more in line with this meaning of the word. In fact, it is the second meaning of friend that John used as he wrote his story for his readers. To those readers, a friend was not the buddy that we might envision, nor was a friend quite as close and intimate as we have described. The friend that John wrote about, and one who would have been understood by his readers, was not an equal, or even someone you spent much time with. There was a very real relationship but not the one we have pictured so far.

To John's first-century readers, a friend was someone you knew who was in a position above yours, who knew you and would be willing to use their higher position to help you out at some point when you might need that help. They weren't a buddy but they were a friend in high places who could accomplish things you might not be able to accomplish, and get things done you could not get done yourself. You didn't hang out together and probably never shared a meal, but this friend was a connection to something beyond yourself.

You probably have this type of friend as well, even if they weren't the one who came to mind earlier. Perhaps they are in a higher role at work, have a political position, have a more established place in your career path, or are in some position that has access to abilities that you don't have.

You might never call them up just to hang out or chat about the weather. You may not pat them on the back when you see them or share your private, personal thoughts with them. But they are there and have offered to do what they can do to help out if you ever need them. They are a friend.

This was the friendship Jesus was describing to the men sitting around the table that evening in Jerusalem, and the one offered again to us. It's not the warm and fuzzy, good-buddy version of Jesus that we sometimes sing about and see pictured. It is not a Jesus who is our equal, but rather one who has abilities far beyond our own and who has offered to use those abilities to help when we need them, when we pray in his name.

It is also important to realize that if, for example, we have a friend who is in politics and might even work for the president, it does not mean that our friend can do everything for us that the president might be able to do for us. Our friend can do what their name and position will allow them to do. When we ask for something in their name, those limits apply. Could it be that the same thing applies when we pray in Jesus' name? Could it be that the problem isn't that we are not heard or that we are ignored, but perhaps some of the things we ask for are things that only God controls? Could it be that Jesus' role as the Son of God was to reach out to us and offer us all that he offered, still recognizing that some things remain in the hand of God alone? Could this be the reason that sometimes Jesus wept right along with us when the pain became so unbearable?

If we only understand that having Jesus as a friend means he is some kind of a buddy or a pal we can look at as an equal, and the only way he is truly a friend is if he gives us everything we ask from him, we are going to be disappointed and hurt. But if we hear what John wrote was actually describing a different type of friendship, one that might go beyond simply meeting our demands, it might not make full sense or remove all of our pain. But it might give us a glimpse of hope.

And sometimes, a glimpse of hope is enough.

Ascension of Our Lord
Luke 24:44-53

Then he said to them, "These are my words that I spoke to you while I was still with you — that everything written about me in the law of Moses, the prophets, and the psalms must be fulfilled." Then he opened their minds to understand the scriptures, and he said to them, "Thus it is written, that the Messiah is to suffer and to rise from the dead on the third day, and that repentance and forgiveness of sins is to be proclaimed in his name to all nations, beginning from Jerusalem. You are witnesses of these things. And see, I am sending upon you what my Father promised; so stay here in the city until you have been clothed with power from on high." Then he led them out as far as Bethany, and, lifting up his hands, he blessed them. While he was blessing them, he withdrew from them and was carried up into heaven. And they worshiped him, and returned to Jerusalem with great joy; and they were continually in the temple blessing God.

Travel Arrangements

It was an amazing moment. Everything that had happened before now seemed to lead up to this. All of those things — the stories and teachings, the miracles, the cross and the empty tomb, all of those things seemed to come together to create this one moment in time.

Jesus spoke with them, explaining once again how all of these things had to happen for him to fulfill the things his father wanted him to fulfill. He reminded them that repentance and forgiveness of sins was the message they were to carry out and proclaim to the world, and he promised that God would soon be sending them some power from on high. It would be a power that would help them fulfill their mission to spread the word.

The crowd was standing in a large semicircle facing Jesus. They were standing on the hill near Bethany, just across from Jerusalem. Behind Jesus, they could see the temple courtyard and the Roman fortress where so many things had happened. They could just make out the cemetery on the far side of town and that hole in the ground with the empty tomb. All of those things, and all of the amazing power they represented, seemed very small compared to this moment.

Jesus was almost radiant. His robes were a brilliant white and his face was aglow with a look that struck everyone who was there. It almost looked as if there was a light shining directly on him, creating a halo of bright light around his head. It was an amazing site.

Then slowly, with everyone standing and watching in pure amazement, Jesus began to rise. Of everything that had been seen thus far, this was the most amazing moment of all. From the rock on which he had been standing as he spoke with them, he slowly began to float upward. As he arose, the glow around him appeared to brighten and take on a heavenly color.

Then Jesus stopped.

As everyone watched in amazement, instead of continuing to rise upward, Jesus just kind of tilted a bit to the left and actually appeared to be a bit surprised and thrown off-balance by it all. He appeared to shake slightly, and then as if by some unseen force, Jesus began to lean forward, and his body began to do a very slow, but very complete forward somersault in the clouds hanging there over everyone's head.

The technicians behind the scenes at the Passion play were scurrying around trying to figure out what had gone wrong with the lift mechanism, and the other actors on stage were trying to figure out how to maintain some form of dignity and awe, while the lead actor tried to hold his robe in an appropriate manner as he found himself upside down in front of the entire audience. As the curtain was lowered, the orchestra began playing the "Hallelujah Chorus" and a group of angels swooped onto the stage to distract the audience, while a stagehand brought out a long stepladder to help get Jesus back down to earth.

The ascension has always been troubling, hasn't it? Once we get through the intellectual struggle to come to grips with the resurrection, we are then faced with the challenge of the story of the risen Lord, actually being lifted up into the clouds, into heaven. This may have been a bit easier to accept in the days before satellites and our overall understanding of things like astronomy and physics, but today, let's just say it is simply too much for some of us in our faith journey.

In short, the common telling of the story is that Jesus was with his disciples on the Mount of Olives. There is a church there today, marking the spot where tradition believes they gathered. Some traditions claim to know the actual rock Jesus was standing on as he spoke with them. After talking with them for a while, he ascended. He physically rose up, and floated into the sky, returning to heaven to be with his Father. It is one of those things you either believe or do not believe, or you just pretend it never happened and don't talk about it. That way we avoid the problems.

We do have to admit that the idea of someone floating up from a hill in the Middle East and ending up in a physical heaven is very difficult to fit into the rest of the things we know about life in general. The old beliefs about seven layers of physical heaven forming a dome around the earth was set aside many years ago. It seems that if we are going to be able to accept this physical ascension, we are either going to have to argue that what we have learned in the sciences is wrong, or that somehow the real existence of heaven is somehow shielded from view by some heavenly force that protects it from our observation. Both approaches have been taken. This is one of the stories that provides fuel for the strong view that our human sciences stand in direct conflict with a real and true religious faith. The belief is that if we teach these facts of science, we are undermining the very root stories of faith, and that must not happen. Some argue that questioning the stories of faith is dangerous and cannot be allowed. Other groups have no fear of modern science and say that if God wants to hide heaven from our earthly view, God can just do that. That's why heaven does not show up when we go looking for it.

What can we do with this story of the ascension? Is there anything we could say here today that might do anything at all to ease this amazingly divisive conflict?

First, consider this: The stories in scripture never say that anyone actually saw Jesus rise from the ground and float up into heaven. Take a look at today's passage. It says, "While he was blessing them, he withdrew from them and was carried up into heaven" (v. 51). He withdrew from them. This is the same phrase we see many other times when Jesus physically went away from everyone else: to pray in the wilderness, to take his disciples to Caesarea Philippi before going to Jerusalem, and to pray by himself in the garden at Gethsemane. Luke tells us directly that Jesus withdrew from the crowd, to be alone. Exactly when and how Jesus then made his way to heaven is not something Luke actually tells us.

While it is still possible that Jesus ascended exactly as tradition envisioned it, Luke simply points out that it is possible the crowd was not there to see it.

Or consider that what is most important is that whatever the crowds may or may not have seen in the sky, their focus quickly returned to what was going on down here. We are told that as Jesus was speaking with them, he told them that since they had been witnesses to the things he had done, they were now to go out into the world and tell those things. They were to announce that repentance and forgiveness was free for everyone. Jesus told them to stay in the city until they were "clothed with power from on high" (v. 49), so they could do the work they had to do. What is important is that rather than standing there, staring up into the sky, fretting about heavenly things, they quickly returned their focus to the real needs of the world around them.

It is easy to lose sight of what it was that the ascension would have been for. We get wrapped up in trying to prove things that are very difficult for us humans to prove, when we perhaps would be accomplishing more if we focused our view on those around us who are hurting or homeless, and doing what we can to help. We spend too much time worrying about how science might threaten the stories from the Bible, when we could be focusing on how to use that science to figure out how to give water, food, and peace to a starving and self-destructive world. It is sometimes helpful to remember that the God who loves us, loves everybody else on this planet just as much.

Whichever way Jesus made his return to his Father, and wherever that may actually be, the number one thing Jesus is concerned about is how well we are following his clear directive to love one another, rather than arguing over how he made the trip back home.

I have made your name known to those whom you gave me from the world. They were yours, and you gave them to me, and they have kept your word. Now they know that every-thing you have given me is from you; for the words that you gave to me I have given to them, and they have received them and know in truth that I came from you; and they have be-lieved that you sent me. I am asking on their behalf; I am not asking on behalf of the world, but on behalf of those whom you gave me, because they are yours. All mine are yours, and yours are mine; and I have been glorified in them. And now I am no longer in the world, but they are in the world, and I am coming to you. Holy Father, protect them in your name that you have given me, so that they may be one, as we are one. While I was with them, I protected them in your name that you have given me. I guarded them, and not one of them was lost except the one destined to be lost, so that the scrip-ture might be fulfilled. But now I am coming to you, and I speak these things in the world so that they may have my joy made complete in themselves. I have given them your word, and the world has hated them because they do not belong to the world, just as I do not belong to the world. I am not ask-ing you to take them out of the world, but I ask you to protect them from the evil one. They do not belong to the world, just as I do not belong to the world. Sanctify them in the truth; your word is truth. As you have sent me into the world, so I have sent them into the world. And for their sakes I sanctify myself, so that they also may be sanctified in truth.

Making Sense

Have you ever come across a piece of scripture that you really just didn't know what to do with? Everything you read before it makes sense, and everything after it, but that one passage just sits there staring at you, almost defying you to understand why it is there and what it means.

We may have that problem with today's passage from John's gospel. John is describing the things that happened while Jesus and the disciples were around the table celebrating the Passover seder on the night before he was arrested. When the meal was over and Judas had run from the room after being identified as the betrayer, Jesus talked with them for quite a while. He seemed to understand this was his last opportunity to teach them and help them understand. He told them not to let their hearts be troubled, but just believe in him, and in God, and all would work out. He talked about his love for them, and how they should love one another. He told stories like the one about him being the true vine. He warned them that he soon would no longer be with them as he had been, but they should not be afraid, comparing what was to happen to a woman giving birth to a child. There would be pain, but then everyone would celebrate when they saw what was actually borne from that pain.

Jesus was trying very hard to help the disciples understand what he was saying, and at one point they actually said to him, "Yes, now you are speaking plainly, not in figures of speech! Now we know that you know all things." The disciples had always struggled with the many parables they had heard him tell and seemed to do much better with this "tell it like it is" approach. We can almost see them all smiling and looking at each other, excited about the fact that they were finally understanding what he was saying. But then, right after they said they were beginning to understand him, Jesus paused, and we're told he looked upward toward heaven as he began praying.

And this is where it seems a bit puzzling.

After trying so hard to speak in a way the disciples could understand, he sat with them and offered a prayer that included, "I am asking on their behalf; I am not asking on behalf of the world, but on behalf of those you gave me, because they are yours. All mine are yours, and yours are mine; and I have been glorified in them. And now I am no longer in the world, but they are in the world, and I am coming to you" (vv. 9-11). And he ends his prayer with, "I made your name known to them, and I will make it known, so that the love with which you have loved me may be in them, and I in them" (v. 26).

Why the huge change in language? After speaking so casually to help the disciples understand everything, why would Jesus become so formal when he prayed? In less than an hour he would kneel in the garden of Gethsemane and pray: "Daddy, if you can get me out of this, please do!" It wasn't that Jesus believed that he had to speak in a highly formal way when he prayed to God. So why?

In my imagination, I see the smiles disappearing from the faces of the disciples as Jesus began his prayer. Once again, they were lost. They just didn't understand. He was speaking so clearly before, but not now. Why?

I have a particular reason in mind for looking at the many people who have made a personal decision to look more closely at their faith. As a part of that decision, they set a personal goal to spend time each day reading the Bible. Their goal is to read every day until they have read the entire story of the faith. They get started and things go very well until the day they run into a passage like this one in John; one that seems to defy them to understand what it says. In almost every case that is the day they stop reading. There is usually one of three reasons they actually stop. Either they aren't capable of understanding the great mysteries of the word of God, the Bible is just too old to make any real sense today, or the Bible is just kind of thrown together with no real design and no real way to sort through it all to make any sense. If we can help make some sense of this strange little passage, perhaps it will help someone keep reading when they run into it, and others like it, in the future.

Because the passage *does* make sense.

What we want to remember is that each of the gospel writers was writing at a specific time, to a specific audience. John wrote his book later than the other writers, and during a time in which the early church was facing some really horrendous challenges. The church had become visible enough to get the attention of the Roman leaders, and their response was to begin some profoundly harsh acts of persecution. They also worked to keep new converts from joining the church and to destroy those who already professed to be followers of this Jesus of Nazareth. Much of what John wrote was aimed at those persecutors or at those who needed encouragement to take the huge risk to become a part of the new church.

Even more disturbing were the arguments that had developed within the church itself. As much as Rome damaged the church by discouraging converts, this internal battleground served to divide and split the new church into pieces, further weakening it to the point of threatening its very survival. John wrote many of his words to ease this internal fighting and that is what we find him doing in this passage we are talking about today. The things the early church fought about may sound strange to us today, just as our current religious arguments would be strange to them. They argued about numbers. The Bible talked about God, Jesus, and the Holy Spirit. Did that mean there were three different beings or were they all actually one being who appeared at different times? It may not sound all that important to us, but it was enough to divide the small early church into different factions at the time. And was Jesus truly fully human, or was he partly God and partly human, or was he fully God and only appearing to be human? Again, it sounds like the topic of a seminary class today, but then, it sparked the creation of several other branches of the Christian church.

These are the kinds of arguments that develop as the church spreads into different places with very different beliefs and cultures. Our passage today is based on an argument that arose as the early church began to grow in the highly intellectual cultures of Greece and Rome. These were also the seats of the origin of things like logic and law, so this new Christian faith was viewed through those filters. The argument went like this: Even if we do accept the story that Jesus lived on earth, died on the cross, and was fully resurrected as the stories say, how does that give him the authority to be the one who can forgive sins? According to the law of the day, forgiveness of any crime could only be granted by a supreme judge who had the ultimate authority to grant such forgiveness. It was clear that even Jesus admitted that God was the ultimate judge, and he was only the Son or servant of the judge. How could anyone possibly have his or her sins forgiven by being a follower of the servant of the judge?

For John's reading audience, the one thing that made the new church so difficult for people to accept was the fact that it was not logical; it argued that sins could be forgiven by the servant, rather than by the supreme judge. No matter how wonderful a story John told, it was meaningless unless he could somehow resolve this issue of the forgiveness of sins.

With that in mind, we can close our eyes and imagine Jesus no longer sitting at the table with the disciples but standing in the courtroom, making his closing statement before the jury. While the words before and after the prayer were to help the disciples understand, John wrote the prayer to make perfect sense to those logical Greeks and Romans.

In a formal, structured manner, Jesus stated his case in his prayer. He recognized that God is supreme and that everything and everyone belongs to God. He then made the affirmation that he, Jesus, actually came from God and that he was acting on God's behalf. He was not a servant but the earthly representative of the supreme judge with full, legal authority to care for those God has given him. While we read through these words, scratching our heads and trying to make sense of the language, John's audience would have read it in amazement, for the first time finding the logical argument that made sense to them and clarified just who this Jesus actually was. John was not writing to us here but taking the opportunity to talk directly to those first-century logicians, with the hope of avoiding another destructive split in the church. As soon as he made his point, he wrote: "After Jesus had spoken these words, he went out with his disciples across the Kidron valley" (John 18:1).

Sometimes things just may not make sense to us, simply because they weren't written for us. And rather than close the book, we simply turn the page, and wait for the writer to look back in our direction and speak to us.

It's always worth the wait.